THE ARCHITECTURE OF
LAW COURTS

Jon Wallsgrove

October 2019 revision
First published in 2019 by Paragon Publishing

© 2019 Jon Wallsgrove

The rights of Jon Wallsgrove to be identified as the author of this work have been asserted by him in accordance with the Copyright, Designs and Patents Act of 1988.
All rights reserved; no part of this publication may be reproduced, stored in a retrieval system, or transmitted in any form or by any means, electronic, mechanical, photocopying, recording or otherwise without the prior written consent of the publisher or a licence permitting copying in the UK issued by the Copyright Licensing Agency Ltd.
www.cla.co.uk

ISBN 978-1-78222-702-1

Front cover photos: Sunderland justice centre, Manchester Civil Justice Centre, Newport IoW justice centre, Bristol magistrates, Bristol civil courts, Westminster magistrates. Rear cover photos: Bristol Civil courts, Aberystwyth justice centre.

All photographs in this book, except for the ones credited
in appendix 5.1, are owned by the author.

Book design, layout and production management by Into Print
www.intoprint.net
+44 (0)1604 832149

CONTENTS

1. **INTRODUCTION** 6
   - 1.1. A brief history of law courts in England and Wales 6
   - 1.2. Law courts in the 21st century 24
   - 1.3. The future of law courts 34

2. **DESIGN PRINCIPLES FOR LAW COURTS** 36
   - 2.1. The ten key fundamentals of law court design 36

3. **FROM FUNDAMENTALS TO FUNCTION TO ARCHITECTURE** 38
   - 3.1. Context
     - 3.1.1. Site planning 41
     - 3.1.2. Urban design/townscape 43
     - 3.1.3. Landscape design 44
     - 3.1.4. Extending existing buildings 49
     - 3.1.5. Reusing historic buildings 51
     - 3.1.6. Environmental sustainability 76
   - 3.2. Form
     - 3.2.1. Form and massing 77
     - 3.2.2. Building plan forms 79
     - 3.2.3. Appearance, aesthetics and architecture 83
     - 3.2.4. External spaces 89
     - 3.2.5. Major internal spaces 91
       - 3.2.5.1. Entrances 91
       - 3.2.5.2. Court Halls 93
       - 3.2.5.3. Courtrooms 97
       - 3.2.5.4. Circulation spaces 102
       - 3.2.5.5. Retiring rooms 103
       - 3.2.5.6. Consultation rooms 106
       - 3.2.5.7. Offices 107
   - 3.3. Detail
     - 3.3.1. Architectural scale 113
     - 3.3.2. External detail 118
     - 3.3.3. Interior design 121
     - 3.3.4. Interior materials 124

- 3.3.5. Internal detailing 126
- 3.3.6. Colour 127
- 3.3.7. Environmental quality 130
- 3.3.8. Appearance of security features 132

4. Portfolio of examples
4.1. New court buildings 2000 - 2015
- 4.1.1. Cambridge County court 135
- 4.1.2. Manchester magistrates 136
- 4.1.3. Huntingdon magistrates 138
- 4.1.4. Worle magistrates 141
- 4.1.5. Exeter crown 142
- 4.1.6. Bristol magistrates 144
- 4.1.7. Cambridge Crown 146
- 4.1.8. Loughborough magistrates 148
- 4.1.9. Cambridge magistrates 150
- 4.1.10. Manchester Civil Justice Centre 152
- 4.1.11. Salisbury magistrates 157
- 4.1.12. Caernarfon criminal courts 159
- 4.1.13. Leamington Spa Justice Centre 161
- 4.1.14. Bristol Civil Justice Centre 165
- 4.1.15. City of Westminster magistrates 167
- 4.1.16. Chelmsford magistrates 170
- 4.1.17. Colchester magistrates 172
- 4.1.18. Newport magistrates 175

4.2. Restored, extended, reused courts
- 4.2.1. Manchester Minshull St Crown Court 179
- 4.2.2. Dundee Sheriff court 185
- 4.2.3. Derby magistrates 186
- 4.2.4. Liverpool Community court 190
- 4.2.5. Guernsey Royal courts 192
- 4.2.6. Gee St civil courthouse 194
- 4.2.7. Hendon magistrates 197
- 4.2.8. The Supreme Court 200
- 4.2.9. Isleworth crown 207
- 4.2.10. Aberystwyth Justice Centre 210
- 4.2.11. Sunderland magistrates 213

4.3. Courts to come and the ones that got away
- 4.3.1. Aberystwyth Mill St 216
- 4.3.2. Bradford magistrates 216
- 4.3.3. Aylesbury crown 217
- 4.3.4. Snaresbrook crown 218
- 4.3.5. West Bromwich magistrates 218
- 4.3.6. Sunderland Justice Centre 219
- 4.3.7. Liverpool magistrates 220
- 4.3.8. Birmingham magistrates 222

5. APPENDICES
- 5.1. List of illustrations 223
- 5.2. Data table 228

Introduction
1.1 A brief history of law courts in England and Wales

The core requirements of a law court building derive from the function of carrying out justice. In England, this function has not changed for over 1000 years. The physical techniques and design details for overcoming the perennial problems have changed with time, and will continue to do so, but the group of people talking, listening and deliberating will always remain the fundamental of a court of law.

A recorded description of a law court from the mid 12th century, under Henry II, includes all the core requirements of a modern court under English Law:

> *"In summer, after hearing mass, the king often went to the wood of Vincennes, where he would sit down with his back against an oak. He would have a carpet laid down so that we might sit round him, while all those who had any case to bring before him stood round about. Those who had any suit to present could come to speak to him without hindrance from an usher or any other person. The king would address them directly and ask "Is there anyone here who has a case to be settled?" Those who had one would stand up. Then he would say "Keep silent all of you, and you shall be heard in turn, one after the other." Then he would call Pierre de Fontaines and Geffroi de Villette and say to them "Settle this case for me." If he saw anything needing correction in what was said by those who spoke on his behalf or on behalf of any other person, he would himself intervene to make the necessary adjustments. Then he would pass judgement on each case."*

The core requirements are all there:
- the king as judge controlling the court;
- the judge sitting at the symbolic head of the court and seeing everything;
- the advocates sitting in a formal spatial relationship in front of the judge, but standing to speak for each side;
- the proceedings recorded;
- the parties involved in the case standing around beyond the seated advocates and judge;
- the public standing around the proceedings and able to come and go at will;
- the judge protected, but the ushers not preventing access by the public to the judge and the justice he provides;
- all parties permitted without fear to bring their case to the judge for justice

Henry II (1133 – 1189) established the English system of law courts with trained officials that we know today. Inspired by the courts of his wife, Eleanor of Aquitaine, he sent out travelling judges, the King's Bench, who brought the Common Law to all parts of England. This established laws that, though based on ancient pre-Norman law, were consistent across the country, and not determined by the local feudal lords and their sheriffs. The feudal trial by battle to determine guilt was replaced with a system of juries and fines.

The feudal laws in Wales, known as the 'Laws of Hywel Dda', which varied from place to place, were only replaced by the common English Law nearly 400 years later.

From about 1000 AD to about 1400 AD courts were held in a royal palace or manorial hall or a guild hall. With regard to the architecture of the courtroom there was no fixed furniture, just the dais for the local lord, used by the judge. The climate in England did not encourage out-door courts, as described in the English holdings in France. Oakham Castle (fig 1.1) is the last surviving example of this form of courtroom.

Fig 1.1 Oakham Castle – the earliest form of courthouse with pre-Norman origins

Between about 1400 and 1650 lawyers and the recorder came to sit on benches around a large central table in front of the judge on his dais. The benches had high backs, largely to prevent draughts in the large halls. Witnesses, defendants etc leant over the backs of the benches, to listen and take part. Chester consistory court (fig 1.2) of 1635 is a surviving ecclesiastical example of this standard court design, which lasted for over 250 years. No civil or criminal courtrooms survive from before or during the Commonwealth.

Fig 1.2 Chester consistory court – the standard arrangement until the Commonwealth

Following the restoration of the monarchy in 1660, after the Civil War and Cromwell's rule, purpose designed law courts started to be built. The royal coats of arms in a courtroom (which symbolise that justice is being carried out in the courtroom under the authority of the Crown, not of Parliament) date from the Restoration of the Monarchy. The courtroom architecture echoed the less austere approach to interior design of the English Baroque.

From the Restoration to the Georgian period the amount of fixed furniture in court rooms increased. This was associated with the requirement of each county to provide the accommodation for the hearings and for the touring judge. The courthouses tended to be in the County town. New courthouses tended to be associated with the County Hall, as centre of administration, or with the County gaol. The witnesses, defendants, jury etc were provided with seats, with the public still milling around the hall. The seats for the witness, defendants and jury were on a raised floor level to see over the backs of the advocates benches. The Civil (Nisi Prius) and Criminal (Crown) court layouts were slightly different, and separate fixed furniture layouts were often built at opposite ends of the great hall, enabling the public to move from one case to another. The formal seating installed in the medieval Winchester great hall (fig 1.3) in 1764 is an example of this.

Through this period new courtrooms (There were usually a pair of courts) gradually came to be built as a bay off the side or end of the hall, so as not to interfere with the other functions carried out in the hall, when the courts were not in session. (Judges sat for 2 or 3 days every quarter, with magistrates' Petty sessions in between for a few days.) Eventually these became screened off to prevent the noise and disturbance of the crowd in the hall, which quickly led to them being completely separate rooms off the hall. Warwick Shire Hall (fig 1.4) of 1753 is a good example of this, where the screen had become a wall by 1768.

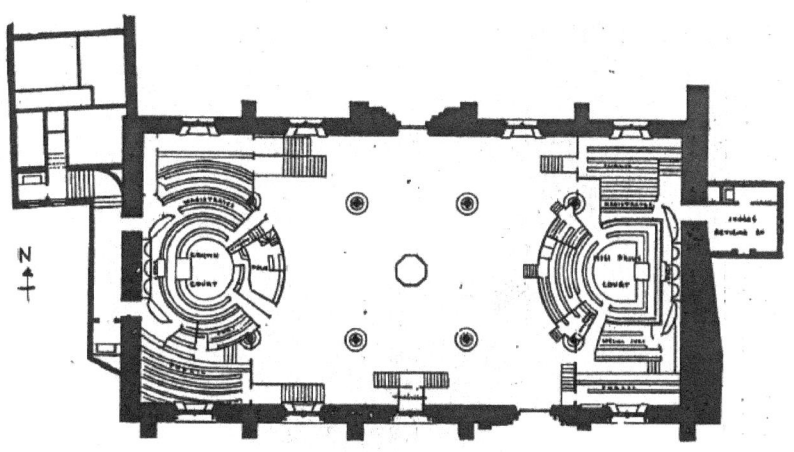

Fig 1.3 Winchester Castle Assizes in 1764 with fitted furniture for civil and criminal courts at opposite ends of the Great Hall, the most common arrangement after the Restoration of the Monarchy

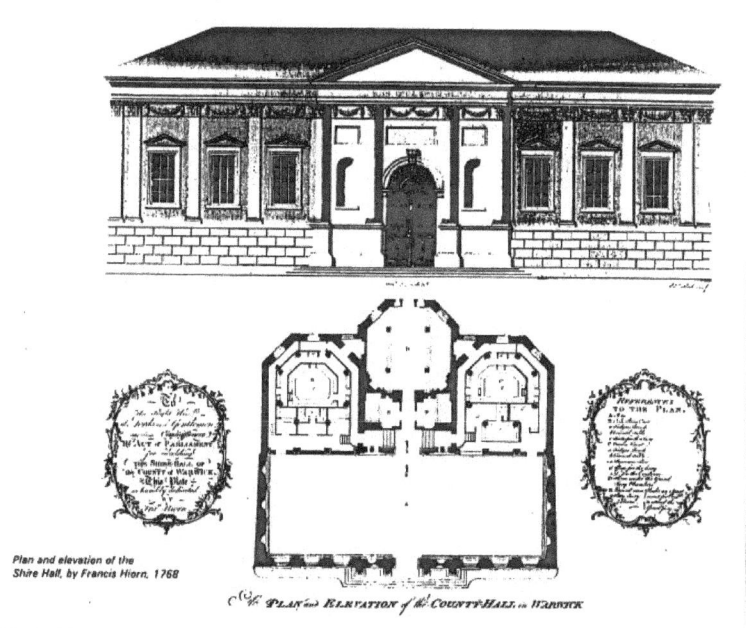

Fig 1.4 Warwick Shire Hall in 1768, with the courtrooms separated from the hall

During this period the judge was also provided with a retiring room and separate access to the building, so that he could not be threatened or influenced by anyone. The dock for the defendant was usually in the middle of the court room, facing the judge beyond the advocates table, and accessed from the cells below, via a secure staircase, as at Ely (fig 1.5), built in 1821.

Fig 1.5 Ely courthouse 1821, built following Corn Law riots, has complete separation of the judiciary from the public, with all parties in fixed seating.

Once the court room was separated from the hall, which became the norm from c.1820 to c.1880, space needed to be provided for the public in the courtroom. To achieve the necessary sightlines over the tiered seating around the well of the court, the public gallery tended to be a balcony over one end or around 3 sides of the court room. Initially the public stood, but later seating was provided to reduce disruption, as at Gloucester (fig 1.6) in 1815.

For the recovery of small debts, from about 1700 to the middle of the 19th century Courts of Request or Courts of Conscience were established. Legislation in 1846 formally established the County Courts in England and Wales to allow a national system for the recovery of small debts. The country was divided into 60 districts, in which one or more purpose designed courts would operate. Each district had a judge who was an experienced barrister, and initially could hear cases up to £20. At first County courts had a jury of 5 members (increased to 8 in 1888). Each court would have a clerk, a bailiff and a treasurer. Existing buildings could be used, but the bulk were built new to the designs of the Surveyor to the County Courts, who was Charles Reeves from 1846 to 1866, then Thomas Charles Sorby from 1866 to 1870. These can be recognised by their Italianate classical style, with offices on the ground floor and usually a single courtroom on the 1st floor and occasionally further offices in the attic storey (fig 1.7).

Fig 1.6 Gloucester Crown Court 1815 has two semi-circular courtrooms with a continuous public gallery to observe the proceedings

Fig 1.7 Burton upon Trent County Court, a typical Charles Reeves Italianate County Court building

The next significant development in court design came in the late 19th century. With the growth in population, particularly in the cities, the one or two court rooms in the county town were no longer sufficient. Large numbers of courtrooms off a large public courthall became necessary. This in turn required separated circulation systems of corridors and staircases for judges, juries and defendants. Lobbies to the courtrooms were also required due to the noise in the busy courthall, where the advocates met with their clients and colleagues. This generated highly complex buildings to maintain the segregation whilst ensuring adequate light, heat and air everywhere. The courtroom layout itself did not need to change. The Royal Courts of Justice (fig 1.8) in London 1874 are the best-known example of this.

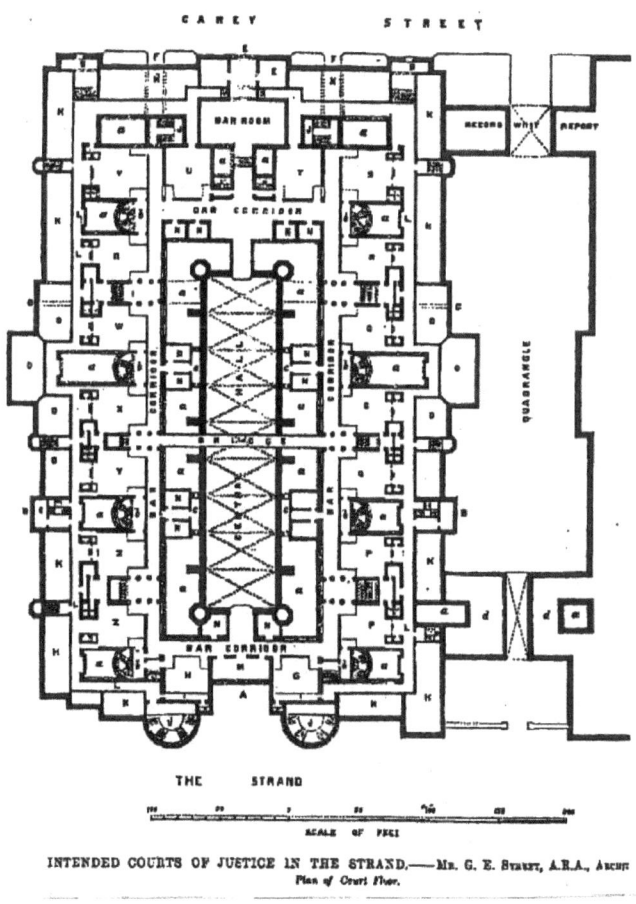

Fig 1.8 The Royal Courts of Justice, London, show the arrangement of a series of courtrooms around a great hall with separate circulation for judges and advocates

They were modelled on the specialist courts attached to Westminster Hall in the Palace of Westminster (fig 1.9), designed by Sir John Soane.

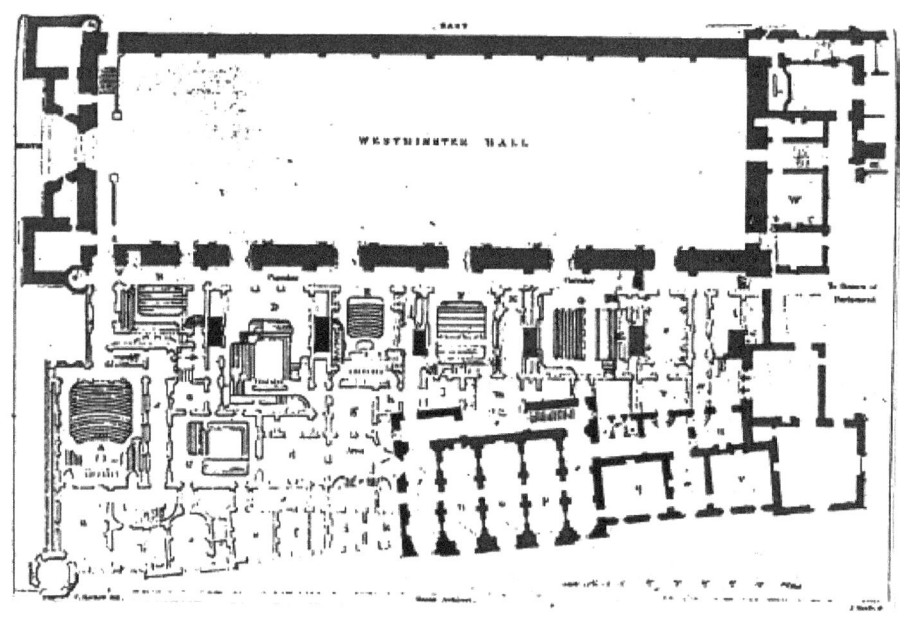

Fig 1.9 Soane's Law Courts built as a series of courtrooms off Westminster Hall, with separate circulation for judges and advocates, which formed the model for all future large court complexes.

The changes from the late 19th century through the 20th century were less to do with changes in the technical form of courts and more to do with the architectural treatment of court buildings. The changes were principally dictated by the influence of local authorities. Since courts were built by local authorities, whenever there was a trend to build new civic complexes new courts came too. This happened in the late 19th century, as population grew and the growth was concentrated in the cities. Birmingham (fig 1.10), Preston (fig 1.11) Liverpool (fig 1.12), Cardiff (fig 1.13) and a great many northern industrial cities built new courts.

The 1930s saw another growth period of court building, often associated with other civic facilities, such as police stations and fire stations. Newport (fig 1.14), Kingston (fig 1.15) and Newcastle (fig 1.16) are examples of this growth period.

(l.) Fig 1.10 Birmingham Assizes, grand civic courts for a new Victorian city
(r.) Fig 1.11 Preston Assizes 1900, a classical civic monument to a great northern city

(l.) Fig 1.12 Liverpool Magistrates' court grew throughout the late 19th century
(r.) Fig 1.13 Cardiff Crown Court is part of an Edwardian Baroque civic complex

Fig 1.15 Kingston on Thames Guildhall has exquisite 1930s detailing, but relegates the magistrates' court to the rear of the complex

Fig 1.14 Newport is a fine example of a 1930s art deco civic complex in South Wales

Fig 1.16 Newcastle magistrates' court is a fine classical street block in the tradition of Georgian Grainger Town, but built in the 1930s and incorporating the police station and fire station as well as the courts.

The final phase of local authority civic building happened after the 2nd world war in the late 1950s and 1960s. This tended to be in the new towns and expanding towns such as Harlow (fig 1.17), Leamington Spa (fig 1.18), and Mold (fig 1.19).

Fig 1.17 Harlow magistrates' court – typical of 1960s new towns

Fig 1.18 Leamington Spa magistrates' court and police station – 1960s neo-classical urbanism for a Regency new town

Fig 1.19 Mold law courts – a bizarre grand stair on a 1960s civic centre

The last fundamental change that affected the design of court buildings was the abolition of the Assizes in 1971. Reform of the system of trial by jury had been discussed since the nineteenth century and by the 1960s the system of itinerant Assize judges, little altered since the Middle Ages, was under severe strain. The amount of cases to be heard was far outstripping the capacity of periodic Assize hearings to deal with them. The number of people on trial tripled in the thirty years from 1938. A Royal Commission headed by Lord Beeching (better known for closing railways) recommended establishing Crown Courts that sat all year around (modelled on the system established in South Lancashire in 1956). These would be concentrated in the larger towns and cities, meaning the abandonment of many smaller county towns where the Assizes had sat for centuries.

Unfortunately, the existing Crown court buildings had been designed to handle far fewer cases, and crucially for only a few weeks a year and Beeching was very critical about conditions: severe overcrowding; little or no separation between the different users of the courts; the cold, the discomfort, the loos, the cramped and primitive holding cells. The judge's accommodation was a subject of particular concern: 'the judge's retiring room may not be much bigger than a cupboard and may, indeed, serve the charwomen in that capacity when its distinguished occupant has gone'. The far greater facilities required for year-round sittings were generally not available in existing Assize Courts, though many were improved to provide the better facilities.

The response to the problems was the Courts Building Programme, which ran originally from 1972 to 1996 but continued through until 2010. 139 schemes were completed in that time, creating 382 new criminal courtrooms (a net increase of 212). In 1972 the Lord Chancellor's Department assumed responsibility from the local and county councils for the provision of Crown Court facilities and the programme was managed by the Property Services Agency (PSA), as at Preston (fig 1.20).

Fig 1.20 Preston Crown Court 1980

A number of key new requirements were incorporated in all new court buildings. Of greatest importance was the requirement for strict segregation of the principal users inside the court: judges, defendants, jurors, vulnerable witnesses and the public and advocates. Segregation was the key element of the increased security measures embedded in every aspect of these new courts. The need to keep these groups in separate areas with separate access to every courtroom created very complex planning requirements. Until then, this had only been necessary in the largest complexes, such as the Royal Courts of Justice or the Old Bailey or the Birmingham Victoria Law courts, and even then the levels of separation were not as thorough.

The other key change to the nature of court buildings was that far more extensive support accommodation was required, for such things as separate waiting and dining areas for the different groups and numerous consultation and meeting rooms.

These changes from the Courts Building Programme did not fundamentally change the courtroom itself. These PSA designs saw the steps in the courtroom floor level reduced or omitted, and the central advocates' table removed and replaced with separate tables. The internal appearance tended to be more open. Light-coloured woodwork was favoured over dark hardwoods. There was a short-lived preference for air conditioned internalised courtrooms with no natural light. The iterations in design development within the courtroom become increasingly minor. The fundamental change was within the rest of the building – bigger complexes, more office space, more support space.

Initially the PSA commissioned designs that were architecturally hard, aloof, brutalist and visibly secure, such as Liverpool QE2 courts (fig 1.21) and Bristol Magistrates Courts Fig 1.22), but they soon matured into softer more welcoming and urbane buildings such as Northampton Combined court (fig 1.23), Lincoln Magistrates' Court fig 1.24) and Truro Crown Court (fig 1.25). Fundamentally the late 20th century saw the move away from an architecture expressing authority and power towards an architecture expressing equality and justice.

Fig 1.21 Brutalism – Liverpool combined

Fig 1.22 Brutalism – Bristol

Fig 1.23 Northampton Crown

Fig 1.24 Lincoln magistrates

Fig 1.25 Truro courts – quality of light and space in the courts building programme

1.2 Law courts in the 21st century

The changes to law courts in the 21st century derive from a process that started in the late 20th century. There was a policy move away from law courts being provided by local authorities and the police (though funded by central government) towards being provided by central government. The Crown Courts moved in the 1970s, and were often combined with County Courts. This was under the auspices of the Lord Chancellor's Department, which on 1st April 2003 was restructured as part of the modernisation of the Justice system to become the Department for Constitutional Affairs (DCA). It reflected the greater emphasis on constitutional matters and human rights. The Wales Office, the Scotland Office, and the Office of the Advocate General for Scotland (OAG) became located within the new DCA. The principle of establishing a Supreme Court, independent of the House of Lords, was also part of the remit of the new DCA.

On 1st April 2005, Her Majesty's Court Service (HMCS) was formed from the merger of the Court Service and the Magistrates' Courts. This was the operating arm of DCA. The Magistrates' Courts came under the direct responsibility of DCA, being transferred from the Local Authorities, though there had been close cooperation for two years. Where the courts were freestanding, the ownership transferred to DCA. Where they were part of a larger building, a lease was granted. Tribunals and the Coroner's Courts transferred from other Government Departments to come under the jurisdiction of DCA in April 2006, with rationalised working already taking place.

On 9th May 2007 DCA was renamed the Ministry of Justice and took over responsibility for prisons and probation from the Home Office. The creation of MoJ reunited the courts and prisons that had been separated by the 1887 Prisons Act, although they were operated by separate operating organisations – HMCS and NOMS (National Offender Management Service). The functional logic was that all areas of the country could have facilities of equal quality, and all people could have equal access to justice. The financial logic was that different types of courts could share facilities so as to reduce overheads.

The result was that outdated and tired buildings could be replaced by being merged with other court types in the locality, e.g. at Ludlow, where the County Court located over a shoe shop moved into the medieval Guild Hall to share with the magistrates (fig 1.26). Alternatively, a new building could be built to accommodate a number of types of courts, such as Caernarfon (fig1.27), Leamington Spa (fig 1.28), Sunderland, and the historic Bow Street magistrates' court (fig 1.29) which moved into Westminster.

Fig 1.26 Ludlow County Court shared the magistrates' mediaeval Guildhall

Fig 1.27 Caernarfon Crown court moved out of the Georgian Guildhall to share with the magistrates

Fig 1.28 the courts from Warwick, Stratford and Leamington joined the police in a new complex in Leamington Spa

Fig 1.29 Bow Street magistrates' court

The dominant justification for new buildings however was the replacement of multiple older court buildings of the same type in the same vicinity into a new purpose built court building. Examples of this would be Bristol magistrates' court (fig 1.30), Bristol Civil courts, Gee Street civil courthouse, City of Westminster magistrates' court, Huntingdon magistrates' court, Chelmsford magistrates' court, Colchester magistrates' court, Cambridge Crown court, and Manchester Civil Justice Centre (MCJC) (fig 1.31).

Fig 1.30 Bristol Guild hall courts   Fig 1.31 the old Manchester county court

A reason for replacing a court building peculiar to this period was a developer wanting to redevelop the site of a court building as part of a larger development, and thus offering a new court building. This happened at Cambridge magistrates' court, Manchester magistrates' court and Bradford magistrates' court (fig 1.32).

Fig 1.32 Bradford magistrates

Whatever the reason for the new court building, it enabled modern best practice and new legislative requirements to be incorporated. These changes tended to be for the Disability Discrimination Act, which required access by wheelchair to the functions of the court, the Human Rights Act, which required defendants to not be seen entering the building from the street in handcuffs, and the requirement for witnesses to be able to give evidence without having to meet the defendants or their friends in the public courthall. Security scanning at the entrance to prevent weapons being brought into court also had a significant effect on court house design.

In the early 2000's there was a cultural change in the attitude to design of law courts. Lord Falconer, the Lord Chancellor, chaired the Government's Ministerial Design Champions committee. In the 1990s design excellence had been seen by the Government as a way of promoting British industry abroad. For instance, excellence in bridge design, promoted by the Highways Agency, had promoted the civil engineering industry so that they dominated internationally by the end of the decade. The Lord Chancellor was keen to use design excellence in court buildings to promote not only the excellence of public buildings and the British design industry, but also to promote the use of English Law for international civil cases. This not only boosted the law as a significant foreign fee earner, it also promoted the English legal system and democracy in countries where they were updating and modernising their legal systems, e.g. Albania, Australia, Ghana, the Maldives, Eastern Europe and the Middle East. Emulating the Victorian precedent (fig 1.33), a design competition was held for the Manchester Civil Justice Centre. This was a key element in this push for design excellence.

Fig 1.33 Manchester Assize courts competition design 1862

New magistrates' courts buildings promoted the benefits of the magistrates' courts transferring from local to central Government. The design of the Supreme Court (fig 1.34) had to achieve the balance between architectural tradition as fine as the House of Lords and the best in modern functionality and craftsmanship to persuade the Law Lords to move from their home in the Palace of Westminster. Design excellence was seen as a way of overcoming local opposition to change.

Fig 1.34 Supreme court library – balance between new and old

Under the auspices of the Ministerial Design Champions, a Better Court Buildings Action Plan was developed in 2002. It included various aims including:

- Experienced and enthusiastic staff

    The Court Service (now MoJ) has, since responsibility for construction projects was devolved to Departments in the 1970s, had an in-house architect to ensure high architectural standards. Both the current and previous architects have been keen to achieve the best design, through giving advice to designers and project clients. They have many years' experience at not only designing buildings of excellence themselves but also at advising Government Departments on how to achieve this. A key part of their role has been to enthuse internal and external clients about the possibilities and benefits of good architecture. Educating everyone to realise they do not have to accept inferior buildings ensures everyone feels confident to demand the best and reject the second rate.

- Encourage the best designers to become involved in civic buildings

    The only way to get excellent architecture is to use excellent architects. The complexity of court planning requires considerable skill. To turn this complexity into high quality architecture, particularly with difficult sites and historic buildings, can only be achieved by the most talented of architects. Public buildings, including courts have not been the most fashionable or cutting–edge field in which talented designers have wanted to work in recent years. We will encourage the best, most talented and award winning architects to work for us, and develop a strategy to achieve this.

- Appreciating the worth of historic buildings

  A great many existing court buildings have historic value and whilst the support facilities may leave something to be desired, the courtrooms themselves are often very popular amongst the Judiciary and Magistrates. The locations in town centres, and their almost invariable civic quality, are something that is very much sought in modern court complexes. In terms of environmental sustainability there is nothing better than retaining a building that has been there for many decades if not centuries. The natural ventilation and lighting required in modern courts is something usually already present in historic courts. For these reasons the first choice should always be to reuse existing buildings wherever possible. A combination of historic conservation and modern design has the potential to create architectural excellence in the hands of a talented designer.

- Move the balance of design effort from function to architectural quality

  By giving better, clearer and more concise advice to designers and developers we will enable the designers to achieve the functional aspects of the building more easily. This will enable them to concentrate on turning a functional building into high quality architecture, which is our requirement.

The design excellence was achieved using an intelligent client, a clear brief, a procurement system set up to ensure that the best designers were used to design law courts, and sites that challenged the skills of the architects.

It was realised that law courts are one of the most complex of building types that any architect can be asked to design, and the need for city centre sites, but with limited budgets, meant that on top of this the sites are generally the most challenging on which to build anything. Therefore, the Court Standards and Design Guide (CSDG) was rewritten to form a clear brief for design teams. The functional layouts and room relationships were defined, the room layouts and their groupings were provided as CAD drawings ready to cut and paste into schemes (fig 1.35), even the ergonomics of the furniture and an automated Schedule of Requirements were given. This enabled the architects to concentrate on producing Architecture instead of just buildings.

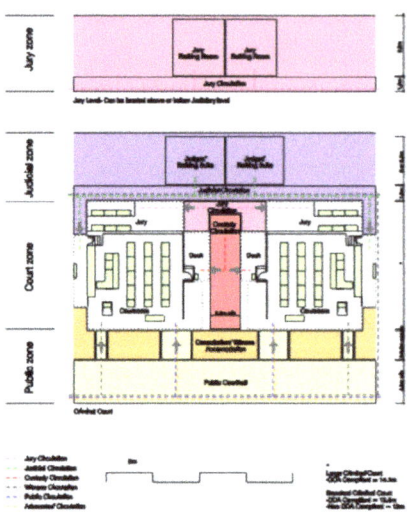

Fig 1.35 plans of courts from the CSDG 2007, ready to paste into a new design

Design teams were selected to be appointed onto a framework contract under OJEU rules. They designed the buildings up to Stage D+ on the RIBA Plan of Work, i.e. developed sufficiently to obtain Planning Permission with sufficient detailed design for the contractor's design team to just need to produce the production drawings. The design was reviewed by an in-house professional intelligent client team (architect, M&E engineer, QS, estates surveyor) at Outline Business Case (OBC) and Full Business Case (FBC) stages to ensure it complied with best practice and was achieving the design excellence required. The client's design team then handed the design over to the contractor and becoming the client's Technical Advisor to monitor the development and construction on site. There were four simple quality selection criteria for the architect:

- The architect shall have designed buildings on difficult and sensitive urban sites.
- The architect shall have designed buildings of similar technical complexity to a court complex.
- The architect shall have designed buildings that have won design awards.
- Where the site is in or affects a conservation area, or includes historic buildings, the architect shall be experienced in the conservation of historic buildings.

This proved remarkably successful in getting the most talented of architects to work for MoJ.

Almost every new court building built since 2000 won a series of design awards. One building, Manchester Civil Justice Centre, (fig 1.36) achieved over 28 design awards, including runner up for the Stirling Prize, the UK's most prestigious design award

.

Fig 1.36 multi award winning Manchester Civil Justice Centre

1.3 The future of law courts

The economic recession caused by the banking crisis of 2008 dominates the future of law courts. It has generated a radical review of the courts estate and of how justice is to be carried out.

Analysis of the number of cases being heard at magistrates' courts and at County courts indicate that these are on a long term declining trend. This is due to the increasing use of on-line civil proceedings and the increasing use of video links. There is also a trend towards a larger number of individual crimes being covered by each case coming to court.

This has led to building closures of underused courts to reduce running costs and achieve capital receipts. 15% of all court buildings are in the process of closure at the time of writing. The rationalisation of office functions, the policy of having no individual offices and 8 desks (subsequently 7 desks, and 5 desks by 2014) per 10 staff and the decline in staff numbers, has enabled the quantity of office space to be reduced and has led to the closure of many office buildings, particularly where leases are expiring and staff can move into court buildings.

This review and rationalisation has effectively reversed the trend since the 1970s of ever increasing back office facilities. The courts are becoming much leaner.

The lull in commissioning new courts has led to a period of review of how future courts should be designed, both with regards to form and process. 10 years of innovative award winning buildings has given some excellent lessons on how to build better courts for the future.

Many possible business plans are being considered, ranging from small targeted works to further rationalise the rural estate to major 36 court centres in major cities, to even reverting to the efficient model of attaching courts to prisons (which had not been seen since the 1870s). The Government policy of "Digital by Default", which was pioneered by small civil claims cases being carried out on line with no need for a courtroom, is leading to more elements of the justice system being carried out on line. However, the lessons are common to all schemes:

Lesson 1: Develop the simple standardised CAD plans of pairs of courts with their associated circulation into a suite of standardised full BIM models of all key court elements that can form the basis of all future court buildings, large or small.

Lesson 2: Use a simple linear plan of repeated pairs of courts, as at Manchester CJC, Aylesbury Crown, and Bristol Magistrates, or the same plan doubled up as at Leamington and Manchester Minshull Street.

Lesson 3: Use low rise buildings to simplify circulation and enable low energy natural light and ventilation, as at Huntingdon, Loughborough, and Exeter

Lesson 4: Extend and convert existing court complexes if large court buildings are needed, as at Manchester Minshull St, Isleworth Crown, Derby magistrates, Snaresbrook Crown

Lesson 5: For smaller courts convert unexpected and economical buildings, e.g. the yacht chandlers converted at Aberystwyth and the glaziers' warehouse converted at Gee St

Lesson 6: Large court complexes give economy of scale, e.g. Manchester CJC, The Royal Courts of Justice, Rolls Building

Lesson 7: Edge of city centre sites give the best balance of affordability, easy access, sustainability and site size availability, for example Sunderland, Cambridge Crown, Caernarfon, Salisbury, Colchester

Overall, the achievement of such a successful award winning portfolio of courts since 2000 gives a strong foundation for whatever the demand for courts might be in the future, both in Britain and around the world.

2. Design principles for law courts

2.1 Ten key fundamentals of law court design

For an architect, law courts are one of the most complex buildings to design. There are numerous separate circulation routes for different users, who must never meet except in the courtroom. The environmental conditions for sound privacy, for a quiet meditative environment, for the fresh cool air to keep people alert on warm afternoons and the air changes to remove the stale odours from the cells are very onerous. The building must express to its users, and to the general public passing by, that the law is important in society and that the decisions carry the ultimate authority, yet at the same time the building must be welcoming to encourage witnesses and for family cases.

The technical requirements are long complex and demanding. However, the designer of a law court building has to see through the complexities to find the fundamental simplicity behind the requirements of a law court. It takes an architect of the greatest talent and skill to achieve a law court building of the simplicity and design excellence required. The following fundamentals are an aid to architects in seeing the clarity of the requirements, and also an aid to clients in assessing whether their designers have achieved what the users of a law court need.

1. The judge (and/or magistrate or jury) must clearly see and hear the advocates, witness and defendant so that they can assess whether they are telling the truth.

2. The public must be able to see and hear what is going on in court, so that justice can be seen to be done. However, they must not be able to stare down or intimidate the witness or judge (or jury), nor must they be able to disrupt the court or threaten the defendant.

3. The defendant must not be able to visually or verbally intimidate the witness or judge/jury. Their line of sight must not be directly facing the witness.

4. The judge, defendants in custody, and public/advocates must have separate entrances and circulation routes in the building, so that they only meet in the courtroom. If there is a jury, they must also have separate circulation from the other three groups, though can share with the judiciary. The court staff can use the judges' circulation. The custody staff will use the defendants' circulation. The advocates will use the public circulation, as will most

witnesses and defendants not in custody. This is all to ensure that there is no possibility of the suggestion of intimidation or influence or of deals being done with the judge or jury.

5. Provision should be made for witnesses who feel that they might be intimidated to avoid using the public space where they might come into contact with either the defendant (when not in custody) or the defendant's supporters. The witnesses should have the possibility of a separate route into the court room where they cannot meet any of the 3 other groups. Alternatively, they can appear in court by video link from another location. This is to avoid justice failing to be done when witnesses are reluctant to give evidence.

6. The plan of the court building should have clarity and be as simple as possible. People using the building for the first time should know where to go without getting lost and without having to resort to large numbers of signs.

7. The building should be easily accessible by all people. It should be convenient for both public transport and private vehicles. This is to ensure that people without their own transport still have access to justice – this could be due to poverty or because they have just lost their driving licence in court.

8. The building should be in a prominent location and be easy to find. This is to avoid unnecessary additional stress when people arrive at a court for the first time.

9. The court building should appear open, friendly and welcoming to reduce stress and encourage witnesses to appear. However, it should also reflect the authority of the law and the finality of the justice dispensed. The serene and welcoming appearance is particularly important for Civil Law and family cases where the judge's decision is about justice and equity, not about guilt and punishment.

10. The building should be recognisable as a law court and be in an important and prominent location in the city or town. This is so that people who never need to use the courts know that justice is there and is important in society.

3. From fundamentals to function to architecture

3.1 Context

It is essential that a wide site search be put in hand when a new building is being considered. A detailed Option Appraisal will be required on at least three sites.

The optimum site area for a court building of any type depends on whether the site is rural or urban, the number of storeys permitted and the number of courts per floor. Although the ideal is to have all courts on one floor level, for practical reasons the number of courts per floor is usually 2, 4 or 6, and. this dictates the number of floors of courts. There has been typically up to one floor of ancillary accommodation for each floor of courts, however in the most efficient new courts this is reducing to one level of ancillary accommodation per two floors of courts. It is expected that this would reduce even further with the introduction of further digital technology and even more flexible working for staff.

Rural and green field sites are now unusual for court buildings, for functional reasons. However, where such sites are viable, the ideal two-storey linear courthall typology can be adopted. The site should be located within 10-15 minutes' walk of more than one form of public transport. The routes to the court by public transport from the catchment areas should be direct and not involve changes or inordinate waits.

In more rural areas access by private car is also of importance. The site must be within 10 - 15 minutes' walk of a public car park for use by staff and the public unless it is in a city centre with suitable public transport from major public car parks. It is also an advantage if the site is close to local solicitors' offices.

Sites in areas peripheral to the town centre are becoming more appropriate as court buildings now tend to have a greater number of courtrooms and the size of the viable town centre is often now shrinking. Courts (particularly Magistrates' Courts) located at some distance from town centres and with poor transport links have an observed tendency for defendants not to turn up. This then generates a need for more arrest warrants.

Good access is important. There should be quick and easy routes for large custody (12m) vehicles and for magistrates'/judges' cars, taxis, etc, to approach and leave the building without delays. A diversity of routes to and from the site is an advantage. Sites in cul-de-sacs, on busy traffic islands, in areas of tight and narrow streets, or adjacent to roads subject to traffic congestion should be avoided if possible. Roads with traffic calming such as humps and chicanes are unsuitable. The minimum access requirement is a 2-way road on at least one frontage with sufficient width to allow a 12m vehicle to turn easily into the site. There must be suitable space and highway requirements to permit a drop-off point for taxis, deliveries (of advocates' papers etc.), and catering supplies (sandwiches) to the public entrance. Adequate provision for deliveries to the secure staff side of the building must also be provided.

The ideal for a medium sized provincial courthouse is a site that is rectangular with a dimension of 55m on the shorter side and with 2-way traffic on 2 or more sides (especially if facing a square or public open spaces). Such site features allow access points for the public separate from the access for judiciary/magistrates, staff, custody and service vehicles. A horseshoe configuration is acceptable, but narrow or waisted sites can tend to be uneconomical, unless the dimensions are fortuitous.

Site dimensions will depend on the number of courtrooms, permitted density, height limitations and the need for an adequate security stand-off distance from unrestricted roads and car parks or other public spaces. (fig.3.1)

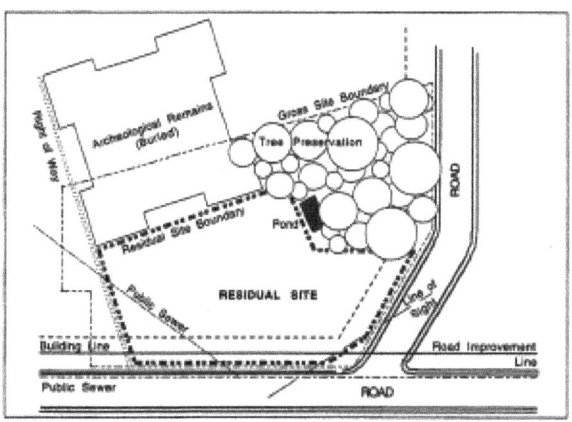

Fig 3.1 site analysis

Existing buildings, particularly if they have strong structures and large spans, can often be used as, or incorporated into, new court buildings. Consideration should be given to the possibility of converting existing buildings if suitable buildings are available. Historic civic buildings and listed buildings often have the appropriate gravitas for a court building. Each courtroom will require a minimum free span space of approximately 7m x 9m. There should be other accommodation on at least 2 sides of such a space, at least 5m width, for use as immediate ancillary accommodation to the courtroom. Existing buildings may also be suitable for the courthall, entrance and ancillary areas, with purpose built courtrooms etc. leading off them.

Historic court buildings tend to have small numbers of courtrooms. Unfortunately, larger complexes of courts are known to be more efficient than many small old buildings, and the space required for modern ancillary functions and separate circulation is rarely present in old buildings. The solution is often to enlarge the best old court buildings by adding more courtrooms and more support spaces. This usually requires the acquisition of additional buildings or land. To make better use of existing buildings, new courtrooms have often been squeezed into spare space. It may be preferable to add complete new groups of courtrooms so that existing space can be stripped out back to its historic structure and better used for ancillary functions and a more rational layout achieved, often by returning to and extending the original planning logic. There are, of course, restrictions on what can be done to a listed building but, in the hands of a talented designer, a combination of historic conservation and modern design has the potential to create architectural excellence.

Derby and Reading area excellent examples of this. (fig 3.2)

Fig 3.2 Reading Crown court – multiple new courtrooms behind historic front

3.1.1 Site planning

The site should be analysed for its relevant features, both within the site and within its context, since these will determine, to a certain extent, the form of the building.

Aspects which should be considered must include:

Views to and from the site
Existing trees and planting
Existing levels
Existing buildings or other structures on the site including archaeology
Landscape context
Townscape context
Topography of the area
Noise
Air pollution
Adjacent buildings and open spaces
Adjacent conservation areas
Scale of local built environment
Skyline
Visual and urban prominence of the site
Solar orientation
Water courses on, below or adjacent to the site
Pedestrian and vehicle access to the site
Relationship to pedestrian routes in the area

The site as acquired may include restrictions and encumbrances that make parts of the site unusable for its main purpose. The removal of encumbrances and addition of planning or building restrictions leaves a useable area or "residual site". (fig 3.3)

The residual site is further constrained by security limitations requiring a "stand-off zone" separating car parking, public roads, and some adjoining structures from the courthouse. Ideally, sites should be sought that can incorporate a stand-off zone of 15m around the building. This zone should be free of places in which a bomb could be concealed. No cars should be able to park in this zone, either on site or on the public highway. Disabled spaces are a particular risk since they tend to be more frequently vacant and always located as close as possible to the entrance; these should never be within the stand-off zone.

However, the ideal is rarely possible and the criteria for the stand-off zone may be relaxed or waived and a similar level of security achieved by other structural and constructional means. The first relaxation to be considered would be to allow Essential Users' car parking within this zone. This will only be allowed where Essential Users' car parking is controlled by a manned gate or other approved security system.

For courts which are designated as low risk, the stand-off zone may be relaxed further.

Special consideration should be given to the hard and soft landscaping and layout to enable easy supervision, to discourage space that could conceal bombs and to prevent damage to the main fabric of the building by accidentally or deliberately errant vehicles (i.e. by the suitable provision of kerbs, bollards etc).

A petrol station, garage or other similar high fire risk building on a boundary would also constitute a risk to the integrity of the courthouse.

The impact of a court building on the neighbouring sites needs to be considered, as does the effect of future development on adjacent sites on the court building. This includes the use of external public space and the proximity to retail and housing. There can be a security risk in courts with custody areas, if there are other tenants in the building, either above or below the courts. They should not share circulation areas. It is preferable for any other users to be below the courts, so that other vertical circulation does not pass through the court levels.

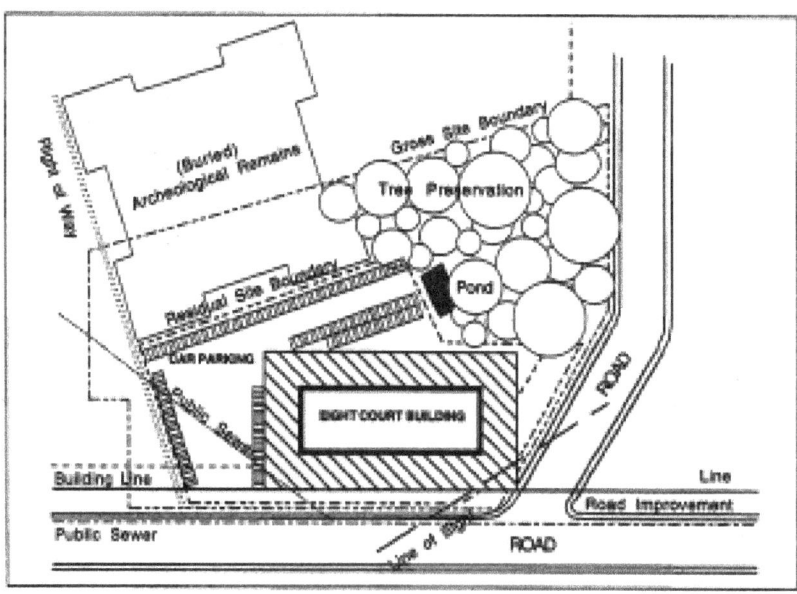

Fig 3.3 residual site

3.1.2 Urban design /townscape

Public buildings such as courts should not only be excellent architecture in their own right, but should also encourage good urban design, so that public buildings contribute to the public realm. A new building should achieve seven principles of urban design, as set out in the CABE publication "By Design" and developed in their "Urban Design Compendium".

- Character – to create a place that strengthens or even creates for the first time that sense of unique identity.

- Continuity and enclosure – to create spaces between buildings that can be as important to the public as the buildings themselves, with a clear distinction between public and private space.

- Public realm – to achieve a quality streetscape with attention to detailed design.

- Ease of movement – to strengthen the urban structure by adding a clear network of connected spaces and routes.

- Legibility – to use landmarks, gateways, focal points, vistas and visual links to help people find their way.

- Diversity – to mix uses to create a continuity of activity throughout the day.

- Adaptability – to make the development adaptable enough to be able to respond to changing social, technological and economic conditions over time.

The courts at Newport on the Isle of Wight (fig 3.4) combine historic buildings and sensitive new buildings to reinstate the important historic townscape where this historic town leads down to the harbour. The post-modern elevations echo the streetscape, and the rotunda turns the corner and defines the end of the street where it meets the waterfront.

Bristol civil justice centre is an example where the building utilises an existing ancient church as a focus to the creation of a new public square opening onto the river frontage. Whilst the courts are functionally the most important building in the square, they choose to take a background architecture to define the space, since it is the square itself that is ultimately the key act of creation in the urban context.

Derby magistrate's court creates a public square within the wings of the old building, but it is clearly defined as a private space for the courts rather than a public street space. Manchester Civil Justice Centre deliberately is a high rise building to simultaneously form a landmark and focal point to orientate yourself within the city, whilst donating a large public area between the courts and the adjacent museum.

Fig 3.4 Newport IoW courts

The Bristol magistrate's court scheme achieves a huge diversity within the city, by being not only a public court building, but also a bus station, a shopping arcade and affordable housing, all set within the context of historic priory buildings.

The City of Westminster magistrates' court achieves the continuity of the streetscape by retaining the small historic corner building to define the edge of the conservation area and projecting the main Marylebone Road façade over the pavement to reinstate the formerly lost street line.

3.1.3 Landscape design

The vast majority of law courts are located in city centres without much scope for landscape design, particularly soft landscape. Most landscape is therefore hard and more associated with townscape.

Kings Lynn Crown court (fig 3.5), Bristol magistrates' court and Cambridge Crown court are examples of minimal and hard landscape around new court buildings.

Manchester Civil Justice Centre and Exeter Crown court have a small amount of soft landscaping as well as hard landscaping.

The Snaresbrook crown court extension (fig 3.6) is a rarity in that it sits within mature soft landscape, and its design is derived from the formal landscape gardens and of the wildness of Epping Forest. The proposed Sunderland combined court not only has a formal garden extending the building, but also exploits a cliff top site overlooking a wild gorge that is probably the most dramatic location ever selected for a new court building.

In principle, what minimal existing landscape is available should be exploited. The large mature plane tree outside the Supreme Court is a key part of its setting, and the retained plane tree outside the Westminster magistrates' courts softens the harsh polluted atmosphere of the Euston Road. (fig 3.7)

Fig 3.5 Kings Lynn Crown court in its historic quayside setting

Fig 3.6 Snaresbrook

Fig 3.7 Westminster

Security is often a key factor in the design of soft landscape. There should be no place for people to hide and thus threaten people attending court, so large shrubs tend not to be suitable. There should be no place to hide weapons or bombs, so shrubby ground cover is undesirable. The security of boundary walls and fences should not be compromised, so trees with low branches and climbing plants should not be used near security walls and fences. Sight lines for cameras and security guards should not be compromised, so no trees or shrubs or climbers can be used abutting the walls of the building. (fig.3.8)

Fig 3.8 Nuneaton

This leaves clear stemmed shrubs, trees with clear trunks, mature trees, low ground cover, grass and bulbs as suitable plants for soft landscaping. Seating, retaining walls, large boulders, sculpture, steps and paving are the other landscaping materials to be used. (fig 3.9)

Fig 3.9 Supreme Court

One of the key landscape designer's tricks is to "borrow" landscape from outside the site as a setting for the court building. Exeter Crown court exploits this well. (fig 3.10)

Fig 3.10 Exeter Crown court

3.1.4 Extending existing buildings

The key factor for a successful major extension is to work with and extend the existing planning logic. If the original planning logic has been lost over time through earlier alterations, then the plans should be studied to understand and revert to the original logic. Demolition of earlier alterations and extensions is commonly required. A confused and convoluted building plan is unlikely to be well received by staff or the public. The entire new complex should read as one building.

There are two fundamentally contrasting approaches than can be taken to major new extensions:

- either conserve the existing courtrooms and add new entrance and back of house
- or add new courtrooms and restore existing building as entrance and back of house.

Most schemes will be principally one approach with elements from the other.

For instance, where there are grand courtrooms, but no original fittings, the space may become the courthall or entrance area with a suite of new courtrooms beyond. Where there are some fine and original courtrooms but squalid support facilities and back office, then a new entrance and support facilities can be built, leading through to the original courts. Often some new courts would also be added in the latter option.

Fig 3.11 Manchester Minshull St Crown court

The first approach is exemplified by Manchester Minshull Street (fig 3.11). This was built in the 19th century as a police court building. It was U shaped in plan with the entrance across the base of he U and eight courts double stacked either side of an open courtyard. The entrance hall was narrow and required all users to climb multiple flights of stairs to circulate anywhere. There was little space for waiting and no space for security. For the conversion, the plan was reversed. The courtyard was glazed over and became the main waiting and circulation area. A derelict warehouse at the rear of the building was demolished and replaced by a new entrance block and additional courts following the pattern of the existing courts. The new entrance had generous space for security and entry was step free for disabled users, and it also faced the rapidly improving area between the station and main city square. All courts were accessed from the new atrium. A new custody area was built under the new entrance wing, giving separate and secure access to all courts. The historic entrance spaces off what had become a narrow backstreet are used only by staff and judiciary.

Fig 3.12 Derby

The second approach is exemplified by Derby magistrates' court (fig 3.12). The original building had developed over many centuries. The main front dated from 1650 and faced a courtyard with the Georgian judges' lodging and hotel forming flanking wings. The main courthall had been altered internally and refitted in about 1780. Behind this were two fine mid Victorian courtrooms. Behind this fine front group were a large array of very poor later courtrooms, offices, inadequate custody areas and circuitous circulation. Everything, apart from the entrance hall, courtyard and flanking wings and the two fine courtrooms, was demolished. A new suite of courtrooms was built in a U shape to the rear of the retained buildings. The historic courthall was restored and used as the main entrance, leading up to a top lit horse shoe courthall that encircles the historic core and feeds into a ring of excellent modern courtrooms.

3.1.5 Reusing historic buildings

The brief outline of the history of court design in the introduction shows that there is no fundamental functional reason why older and particularly historic courts should not be used today. MoJ owns or occupies nearly 700 court buildings, of which nearly 150 are historic buildings and Listed by English Heritage as being of historic or architectural interest. Of the remainder, a considerable number are sound buildings often in Conservation areas and of some architectural or functional merit. MoJ does not have, nor is it ever likely to have, the funds or will to replace all these older buildings. On average over the last 100 years about 5 or 6 buildings are replaced each year.

The economic crisis of the late 2000s led to the disposal of about 20% of the total number of law courts. This has affected historic courts to the same extent as more recent court buildings. The first priorities for replacement are those buildings where the lease has expired and cannot be renewed, or where capital can be raised from a sale, or where cost savings can be made by moving elsewhere. The second priorities are the buildings that are expensive to run in terms of maintenance and energy (typically buildings from the 1950s to 1970s), and buildings that are incapable of providing justice to the public. Historic buildings rarely fall into these categories.

More common amongst historic buildings is that they are small, so that they have a higher number of staff when calculated per courtroom. They also tend to be lacking in some of the facilities required in a modern court building, such as security, witness facilities, custody van docks and facilities for the disabled. The reuse of such buildings therefore needs such aspects to be addressed. It is helpful to understand the common factors of historic court types to aid in their reuse.

County Halls and Sessions Houses

Fig 3.13 Westminster Hall

The earliest type of court buildings were the medieval baronial or royal halls (Westminster Hall (fig 3.13), Ludlow, Oakham Castle, Winchester) which served a multitude of purposes, that included courts for a few days each quarter, or sometimes more frequently. These tended to be mediaeval gothic or vernacular in style. Such buildings later tended to be fitted out with permanent fittings at one (or both) ends of the room, then with a screen to separate the court function from the remainder of the multi purpose hall. This final form then became the model for the Georgian County Halls and Sessions Houses that were built in virtually every county town in the late 18th and early 19th century (York (fig 3.14), Warwick, Salisbury, Derby, Pontefract).

Fig3.14 York Crown Court

These were generally classical in style, with a few in the gothic revival style. Many were built as part of a prison complex, with the court usually fronting the prison (the prison has often long since gone). It was not unusual to locate these new buildings within historic complexes, particularly castles associated with justice - Exeter, Caernarfon, Durham, Lancaster (fig 3.15).

The age of the sessions house or county hall is therefore often not that of the host castle. There were most commonly 2 courtrooms, a Crown Court and a Nisi Prius court. In addition, there was usually a Grand Jury room, which acted as a council room and a pre-trial hearing room. This has very commonly now been turned into a further courtroom, though usually has no link to custody, so is sometimes a county court room or used for non-custodial cases. (fig 3.16)

Fig 3.15 Durham

Fig 3.16 Warwick Crown

Town halls and Guild Halls

In the mid-19th century through to the early 20th century courts tended to be built as part of municipal town hall complexes both large (Leicester, Southampton, Newcastle, Middlesex Guildhall, Bristol Guildhall, Kingston town hall) and small (Ipswich, Colchester, Southampton, Penzance, Brentford). Large purpose built court complexes were also built (Royal Courts of Justice, Birmingham Victoria Law Courts (fig 3.17), Bedford, Cardiff).

Such buildings were varied in style. Where the client wished to express he importance of continuity and history they tended to be gothic revival guildhalls. Where civic importance and respectability was key they tended to be classical, particularly Edwardian Baroque. Where it was felt important to express the dynamic modernism of the borough, art deco tended to be favoured e.g. Newport (fig 3.18).

Fig 3.17 Birmingham VLC

Fig 3.18 Newport Crown

County Courts

County courts were first created in the mid 19th century under the 1846 Act. They were all purpose built by Charles Reeves from 1847 to 1866 and by Thomas Sorby from 1867 to 1876. They were all Italianate classical in style in a formula, and nearly half are still in use.

Halifax (fig 3.19) is a typical example. From 1870 the designs were carried out for the Commissioners of Her Majesty's Works, and County Courts tended to become multi functional. Until WW2 they often included Inland Revenue, Probate Registry, Customs Office and sometimes even the Post Office. Manchester and Ilford (fig 3.20) are typical examples.

Fig 3.19 Halifax County

Fig 3.20 Ilford

POLICE COURTS

Combined police station/court buildings started to be established following the 1835 Municipal Corporations Act, being adopted slowly across the country through the 19th century. Police courts, now known as magistrates' courts, were largely built in the late 19th and early 20th century. The series of London courts by John Dixon Butler are most well known, e.g. Rochester Row (fig 3.21).

The combined police and magistrates' courts buildings were built into the late 20th century by local authorities, until responsibility for the police and magistrates were removed from local authority control in 1995 and 2005 respectively.

Fig 3.21 Rochester Row police court

OTHER CONVERTED HISTORIC BUILDINGS

Many courts housed in historic or listed buildings were not necessarily built as courts originally. A range of buildings have been converted to courts, including town halls, schools, customs houses, police stations, offices, private houses, military buildings and industrial buildings e.g. Penzance county court (formerly a house and then the Ministry of Food) (fig 3.22),

Fig 3.22 Penzance County court

Barrow in Furness (formerly a custom house) (fig 3.23)

Fig 3.23 Barrow in Furness

and Oxford (formerly an early car show room) (fig 3.24).

Fig 3.24 Oxford Combined

20ᵀᴴ CENTURY BUILDING TYPES

Throughout the twentieth century court buildings were built in a range of architectural styles, though the fundamental planning logic did not change. The most common styles include:

Edwardian baroque
Art Deco
Vernacular revival fig (3.25)

Fig 3.25 Banbury magistrates' court

Post war modernism
Modernist Brutalism (fig 3.26)

Fig 3.26 Liverpool QE2

Postmodern Contextualism (fig 3.27)

Fig 3.27 Caernarfon

Improving existing facilities

There are a number of key elements of planning logic that have to be achieved to enable any older court building to be reused or continued in use. These are the public entrance sequence, the separation of circulation routes, separate entrances and secure custodial access.

Public entrance sequence

There is a key sequence of functions that have to be passed through on entry:
entrance lobby leading to
security leading to
entrance hall leading to
court hall leading to
courtrooms

Historic buildings were often not designed with this sequence in mind, and achieving it is one of the first tasks in determining whether an historic building can be continued in use. A common solution is to utilise an adjacent building as the entrance lobby, security and entrance hall, prior to entering the existing courthall. Another solution is to use the existing courthall, where it opens directly onto the street, as the entrance lobby, security and entrance hall, and provide a new courthall beyond in either a new or existing space.

Separation of circulation routes

Separate circulation routes are required for the public, the judiciary, custody, jury, and sensitive witnesses. The only place they should meet is in the courtroom. Not all court buildings have the full range of users however. In order of complexity:

Crown courts require separate circulation routes for public, the judiciary, custody, jury, and sensitive witnesses

Magistrates' courts require separate circulation routes for, the judiciary, custody, and sensitive witnesses

County courts require separate circulation routes for the judiciary and public only

Tribunals require no separate circulation routes since the judiciary share circulation with the public.

However, in future, Civil (County) courts, Magistrates' family courts and Tribunals will generally share the same accommodation and be known as CFT (Civil, Family, Tribunal) courts or the Single County Court. These will require separate circulation for the judiciary and public.

One type of court may be reused as a simpler type to avoid circulation problems.

Separate entrances

For security reasons the following require separate entrances to the building: public (including advocates, witnesses and jury), judiciary and staff (including sensitive and intimidated witnesses), custody.

Historic courts tend to have rather more entrances than would now be required, so some can be closed which means this rarely causes a problem, except for security staffing.

Secure custodial access

Where custody is required in the court building, a custody vehicle must be able to drive up to the building into a secure van dock, where the prisoners can be transferred to and from the custody area of the building without being seen by the public.

This can be a fundamental problem, and solving it depends on land availability. Sometimes levels can be exploited, for instance to gain access into a basement for custody. When adjacent buildings or sites come available the initiative should be taken locally to try to acquire them, if it is known that there is a custody access problem. The solution may be to use the building only for non-custodial courts.

Design principles

Return to original form

The key to any alterations or extensions to an older building is to understand the original form of the building and return to it as a starting point for any new design.

Section 2.2 above is a good starting point for understanding the types of historic court buildings, and their generic layout.

Understand the accretions and changes

Having understood the design of the original core of the building, it is then necessary to understand the accretions and changes over the years. As a rule of thumb buildings tend to have major alterations about 3 times a century, and minor changes about every 15 years. By knowing the original date of construction, the number of changes can therefore be estimated, however some changes remove previous alterations. Some of the changes will have been of benefit and others will have made the building more difficult to use. External factors such as war damage should not be ignored, since even if they have been repaired in the past, there may be underlying faults. Some of the additions might be good elements but sometimes the linkages to the core of the building may be poor, in which case the space between new and old can be a potential area to resolve circulation problems. Alternatively, some extensions may be of greatest benefit as a site for a new replacement extension.

Sequential plans should be prepared by the consultants showing the changes over the years, and the dates and significance of the various works should be annotated on a plan. From this, areas of highest importance for preservation should be marked on the plans, as should areas where some change is acceptable, areas where major elements can be removed and areas that would benefit the historic structure by their removal. This will give a clear idea of where the new works should take place.

Extend the original planning logic

Once the original form and subsequent alterations have been understood the planning logic should be clear. This logic should then be extended to create a unified new courthouse, incorporating the best of the old and creating a new building of excellence that should be better than the sum of the parts.

Principles of current courthouse planning

The basic principles of courthouse planning, should be applied to the site. The site is effectively not only the land, but also the original building and any parts of subsequent alterations that are worthy of retention.

Exploit underused spaces

Sometimes the change necessary to make an existing building more appropriate to current usage does not involve fundamental reconstruction of substantial elements. "Do minimum" should always be the option of choice. However, it often takes a considerable number of complex design iterations to be able to realise that the necessary changes are essentially simple, but only obvious once they have been discovered. Underused spaces are the first places to examine as the key to unlock the improved functionality of the building. These can range from the obvious, such as attics, basements, store rooms, underused courtrooms, old plant rooms, light wells etc. to less obvious areas. These might be former stairs, locked off cells, bricked up vaults, inaccessible voids between extensions, space above false ceilings, former link corridors or link bridges, tank rooms, flat roofs, roof voids, outbuildings, caretaker's apartments, stables or sublet shops and offices. Some of these spaces might be small, in which case they might be used to re-house equipment blocking a larger room. Other spaces may be just a narrow sliver of space, but could be useful for vertical or horizontal circulation, or for service routes. Oversized or large but partitioned rooms can be used for open plan offices, leaving smaller inefficient administrative offices for consultation or witness rooms.

Converting existing rooms to new courtrooms

In the past, the easiest conversion tended to be conversion of a suitably sized room into another courtroom. This is still a good possibility, but can also lead to some very poor courtrooms. The separate circulation patterns should be maintained, particularly for custody. County courtrooms or tribunal rooms can have the judicial escape route into a retiring room or another tribunal room to avoid the need for a separate judicial corridor, but this works best for smaller complexes. Ceiling heights, room proportions and column positions are fundamental to adequate sight lines to ensure that the courtroom works properly. The characteristics of the room should not be forgotten when converting existing rooms into courts. Windows should be kept and used. The judge should not be sitting in an inappropriate location such as a fireplace, (as happened at Bristol Guildhall and Halifax magistrates' court (fig 3.28) until recently).

Fig 3.28 Halifax magistrates; court – the bench is in the fireplace!

There must be adequate space to move around the furniture (particularly near columns) and users should not be tripping over awkward steps or the dais. The acoustics and sound insulation of the room should be suitable. Small matters of detail, such as historically appropriate curtains, lighting and wall finishes can transform an old room from the appearance of being a temporary and tatty afterthought into being a desirable and respectable location for the formal administration of justice. The reuse of refurbished historic pieces of furniture from redundant buildings can be particularly appropriate to furnish empty rooms in historic buildings as courts in an appropriate manner.

Adding purpose built courtrooms

The complexity of the planning of courtrooms and their circulation can often be better achieved by building new courtrooms onto historic buildings. These can either replace existing poor quality converted rooms or can be additional capacity to rationalise a number of local court facilities. Where the fault with the current building is the inadequacy of the current converted courtrooms, this can be the best solution. The former converted courtrooms can then revert to more suitable other functions, such as office accommodation or witness facilities or consultation rooms.

Public spaces and circulation

In some cases, both the courtrooms and the back of house facilities are (or can be made) suitable for purpose, but the public spaces and circulation are unworkable. The solutions here tend to be more complex and become more of a design challenge. Opening up partitioned spaces, adding new stairs and lifts, reopening old doors and windows, exploiting underused spaces (fig 3.29), putting jury or staff circulation routes through basements or attics can all help. Creating new entrances, security, reception and waiting areas through neighbouring properties can also be viable solutions, as can entering from the rear or from a side entrance.

Exploit essential maintenance works

When significant maintenance works are required to be carried out, e.g. rewiring, new roof, damp proofing, new heating system, structural repairs, etc., the opportunity should be taken to consider other improvement works that could be carried out simultaneously to save disruption and cost. A typical example would be where the roof has to be repaired and recovered, then the insertion of roof lights or dormers might create useful additional accommodation in the attics. Where scaffold is required in a courtroom to paint the ceiling, the opportunity could be taken to reopen jammed windows or lantern lights to improve the ventilation, cooling and natural light. When central heating plant is replaced with modern smaller plant, rationalise the plant room areas to free up useful space for other purposes.

Fig 3.29 Royal Courts of Justice; redundant attic refurbished for judge's chambers, with reused historic furniture

Selecting buildings for conversion

Converting and modernising existing court buildings are not the only option. Older existing buildings or leases of whole or parts of new buildings can be acquired to convert into courts. Location is still a key factor in selecting the building for use, as is the cost of the building to be acquired. The cost of converting a smart new office building is not very different from converting an awkward empty shell, but the former will tend to have considerable competing demand, so will be more expensive, e.g. the well located Rolls Building annexe to the RCJ, in the City of London (fig 3.30).

The best buildings to convert into court buildings, particularly custody courts, are deep plan, top lit spaces with high roof void volumes and heavy structure, possibly with some areas of quality or interesting finishes, or an element of civic facade. Examples would be the top floor of former department stores, heavy industrial works, military buildings, warehouses or the top floor of a new shopping centre as at Cambridge magistrates' court. Schools have also been frequently and successfully converted in the past but are now in demand for residential use.

Fig 3.30 Rolls Building RCJ annexe – converted from office building

Office buildings, whilst an obvious choice for conversion (fig 3.31), tend to have relatively low ceilings, rarely have adequate number or location of service cores for Crown or magistrates' courts and almost never have capacity for custody areas or custody van docks. When considering a new office building for use as a court it is best to alter the shell and core to suit courts prior to construction. To ensure that the buildings are lettable as commercial offices if the courts vacate, changes to ceiling heights, floor to floor heights, numbers of entrances, positions of cores or special rooftop volumes are acceptable, but steps in structural floor level, lifts or stairs finishing at different floor levels, unusual column grids or blast proof ground floor facades would not be acceptable for normal institutional office standards.

Fig 3.31 Liverpool civil

Generic problems and solutions

The building is thought to be unsuitable

This is the almost invariable first reaction of people who know the building too well or have suffered from managing the annoying maintenance niggles of the building. The answer is to have a fresh look at the building from someone who is trained to see the potential of buildings. It is not unusual to find that a relatively small but innovative idea can transform the potential of an older building.

Entrance security

The space required for a security arch and search table, plus the space for the public to queue up at peak times to be searched can cause a problem in older buildings. Whilst a security arch should be considered the norm for most court buildings, it may be acceptable for smaller and rural court buildings to use a portable security wand, where the risk is considered acceptable. X-ray facilities are only generally required on the highest security court buildings. The space for security together with the space for a draught lobby is one of the key difficulties that can appear to make the building unsuitable.

Separate circulation

Separate circulation routes are required in older buildings, but there may be scope for some compromise. Compromise on separate circulation routes for custody is unlikely to be acceptable. Jurors can use parts of judicial circulation routes since they are they are escorted from court to jury suite, so interaction with the judiciary can be prevented by careful management. Sensitive and intimidated witnesses can use staff circulation, since they will be escorted, however they must not be able to wander at will in the staff areas. The public do not need separate doors into the courtroom, but it is preferable where shown. In informal courts, tribunal rooms, and County courts there need not necessarily be a separate judicial circulation route. There must however be a judicial escape route into a retiring room or another tribunal room to avoid the need for a separate judicial corridor, but this works best for smaller complexes.

Secure docks

Secure docks are not required in all custody courts or even in all buildings that have custody courts. Sensible management can ensure that cases requiring a secure dock can be heard in a court with a secure dock. Therefore, where there is difficulty in providing a secure dock a careful review should be carried out to see whether a secure dock is actually required in the existing building. It is generally preferable to convert the existing dock into a secure dock. The size and capacity of the secure dock is something that can vary from the standards, depending on local requirements. Where the dock is recessed into a wall at present these tend to be the easiest docks to make secure, and should therefore be the first choice to convert. The existing woodwork of the dock should be re-used wherever possible, and can be extended and remodelled to match. The standard detail of frameless glass has been developed to be a neutral adjunct to existing courtroom interiors. Where required the steel structure can be clad in matching woodwork. In particularly important historic courts a purpose designed metalwork secure dock can be used, but a cage-like appearance should be avoided if at all possible.

Office accommodation

Office accommodation is generally the most flexible of the space in a court building. There has been a total move towards open plan offices to give more versatile staffing and to encourage staff from different court backgrounds to work together in a more integrated way. The spaces created by exploiting underused spaces, can make very interesting, characterful and pleasant offices. Roof conversions and mezzanines within larger volumes can be particularly useful for offices, though consideration has to be made for floor loading (fig 3.32).

Fig. 3.32 Lewes Crown Court – attic converted to offices

On middle-aged office buildings that have been much altered in the past, but may well now be open plan, it is often found that windows and roof lights have been blocked up. Since the efficient use of a building, in terms of space utilisation and energy use, is generally determined by the availability of natural light, all blocked windows and roof lights should in principle be re-instated. This should be borne in mind prior to commencing the space planning.

The precise dimensions of the window wall profile and of columns etc. is critical to the efficient use of the floor plate. Furniture should be selected to fit into the dimensions available to avoid wasting space. It should be noted that in refurbished offices the wall and column profiles can vary from original plan dimensions, due to increased insulation and additional service ducts.

Improving plan efficiency of existing cellular buildings is critical. If the building is a frame structure (standard since the 1950s) the partitions should be removed to create open plan space. If the building has openable windows for natural ventilation, when the building is opened up, refurbished and the windows are replaced, the new windows should remain openable for natural ventilation. This is to ensure that energy usage does not rise, when the aim is to reduce energy usage.

Older office buildings tend to have lower floor-to-floor heights, and when they are converted from cellular to open plan he low ceiling can be very oppressive in such a large area. It is often best to omit false ceilings and use chilled beam features for servicing the offices.

Older framed buildings (pre-1950), especially if they were built as industrial buildings, can tend to have characterful structure. This can be exposed steel, cast iron columns, exposed brick walls or rough chunky concrete, as at Gee Street courthouse. It should be exposed and exploited in the interior design to give a less bland office space than normal. This also tends to give slightly more useful floor area by avoiding boxing everything in or removing redundant boxing in. Such minor additional dimensions can be particularly useful for squeezing in doors and lobbies etc. at pinch points.

Sound lobbies

Sound lobbies to courtrooms are required to prevent noise disturbing the court when people enter or leave the room when the court is sitting. Where the public are not permitted in court, or where cases are very short, people will not enter or leave the room when the court is sitting and/or will not disturb the court. In such circumstances the necessary acoustic separation can be achieved by using a single door (or pair of doors) with the necessary acoustic seals, without a lobby and further doors. Two sets of doors immediately abutting can also be used, opening in opposite directions but without a lobby. However, this does not avoid the disturbance problem since both doors have to be opened simultaneously if there is no lobby. If the existing (perhaps historic) doors cannot be brought up to the necessary acoustic standards by themselves this technique can be used. On existing lobbies and doors, the hinges and closers should be oiled and maintained so that the opening of the doors does not cause a noise disturbance in itself.

Sensitive and intimidated witnesses

Sensitive and intimidated witnesses need a small pleasant room with a view on the staff side of the building. The demand is increasing, not only for the protection of the witnesses, but also to encourage witnesses to appear for the better achievement of justice. Such witnesses will inevitably be stressed and nervous, so comfortable furniture, pleasant décor and a relaxing view will help them keep calm. They will need to be escorted to the room, and this in itself will give a sense of security. A long route to the witness room and its remoteness may be a comfort to the witness (though inconvenient for escorting staff) so this can be exploited to utilise remote rooms in the building.

Inclusivity and provision for the disabled

In principle, courts are almost unique as a building type in that all the users can be managed such that cases can be listed at an appropriate court building. This means that to achieve compliance with the Act, not all aspects of the specific existing building need comply with accessibility. Disabled users can have their case heard somewhere more convenient for their disabilities or can use video links, and staff can come to the disabled user if they arrive for advice or wish to submit paperwork. With good management, inclusivity challenges should not be a justification for the closure of a court building.

Acoustic separation

Acoustic separation can be difficult to achieve in existing buildings, both for noise intrusion from outside the building and for noise intrusion from public areas into the court. However, the heavy construction of existing buildings tends to make room to room acoustic separation comparatively easy. Attention should be paid to sealing voids in ceilings, floors, ducts, fireplaces and partitions since these are common sound routes. Non-original partitions in particular can have very poor acoustic separation. Junctions between partitions and external walls or windows are a common source of noise intrusion.

External noise tends to be from traffic. The peaks of traffic noise tend to be from 08.00 to 10.00 and 16.30 to 18.30 (though local conditions vary), whilst courts tend to sit from 10.00 to 16.30. This needs to be borne in mind when analysing noise surveys. Noise surveys are carried out to determine the need for acoustic treatment to windows in courtrooms or the ability to have opening windows in courtrooms. The figures for the hours when the courts are sitting should be used, not the industry standard, taken across the entire day. This should tend to severely reduce the buildings requiring acoustically sealed windows or double glazing, particularly in smaller towns and rural locations. This can be just as valid for new buildings.

IT

The requirements of the growth of facilities for Information Technology within court buildings can generally be relatively easily resolved in traditionally constructed buildings. Floor voids, ceiling voids and daises tend to be very suitable for running cabling horizontally. Chimneys, service ducts, lift shafts, dump waiter shafts, gas piping and ventilation shafts tend to be very suitable for running cabling vertically. Traditional large central courtroom tables and traditional large tables used for meeting rooms and in former grand jury rooms tend to have the depth suitable for computers and the quantity of modern papers. Traditional fitted clerk's desks tend to have inadequate space, but can often be modified with matching craftsmanship to provide more desk space, dedicated computer space, upstands for power and IT outlets and suitable space for a modern comfortable adjustable office chair. Advocates' desks, particularly with fixed seating, tend to have very narrow desks. Birmingham (fig 3.33) and Worcester (fig 3.34) have examples of such alterations. Upstands or under-bench trunking are ways of bringing power and IT cabling to the advocates desks. Where advocated desks are little more than ledges it may be necessary to reduce the number of rows of advocated benches to give adequate desk and seating space.

Fig 3.33 Birmingham VLC

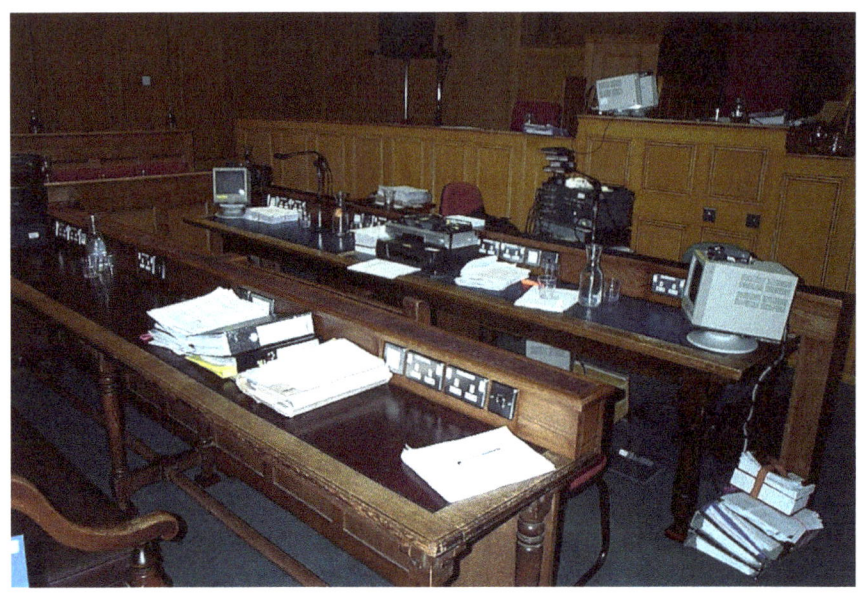

Fig 3.34 Worcester

Heating, cooling and ventilation

Frequently the criticism of the heating, cooling and fresh air in older buildings is significantly down to poor maintenance and lack of understanding of the simple systems. High ceilings and high level windows of typical 18th, 19th and early 20th century buildings (fig 3.35) were designed to allow the hot air to rise then vent out through the windows, using windows on opposite sides to give a cross breeze. The cool fresh air entered through low level vents from an under-floor void or ventilation shaft. Frequently the windows are jammed shut and painted up, with sash cords missing or broken and operating cords, hinges, stays, ratchets and pulleys broken or missing. Similarly, the fresh air vents are often blocked up, painted over of jammed closed, since users claim "they cause draughts". These should all be reinstated and made operable from a convenient position. Powered operation is a possibility if access is difficult. The buildings were often originally designed to have blinds on the windows to prevent glare and overheating, and shutters to reduce heat loss at night and heat gain during the day. These should be reinstated and or repaired. A management system needs to be put in place to operate such systems correctly, and they can be automated and linked to the BMS.

Fig 3.35 York Crown

Open fireplaces would originally have provided ventilation, particularly when lit and drawing air through the room. Although it is unreasonable to have open fires today, the flue can still be used to give stack effect natural ventilation, if the fireplace is vented into the room, and the flue is open at the chimney pots. With the lack of fires to dry out the chimney, care should be taken to prevent water ingress at roof or chimney pot level.

The grander rooms of Victorian public buildings used gasoliers to ventilate large rooms. (fig 3.36)

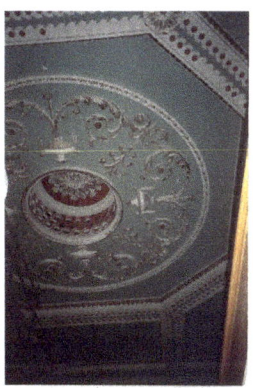

Fig 3.36 Knutsford Crown Court, original ventilation for gasolier reused

A gas-burning chandelier was suspended below a domed or vaulted ceiling, which was perforated with grilles hidden in the ornamental plasterwork. The heat from the gas lights drew the hot air up through the grilles into a duct within the ceiling void and out through a ventilator on the roof. There would usually be grilles at low level in the floor or skirting to draw fresh air in through ducts or the floor void, and are often located to draw air over the radiators. The ducts, grilles and vents often still exist, and sometimes the gasolier (converted to electricity) survives too, e.g. Knutsford. However, the system does not work without the gas lights to power it. Electric fans can be installed in the ceiling duct to bring the system back into use, and the air to the low-level inlet grilles could be chilled or warmed to bring better comfort conditions. The grilles are often painted over and blocked, or covered by carpet if in the floor. Roof ventilators have some times been removed. Any controls or shutters on the louvres or vents are usually broken or jammed. All of this can be brought back into use relatively easily.

Overheating of court buildings in summer tends to be more of a problem than winter cold. If restored existing systems prove inadequate, individual chiller units should be provided in the summer months when it is a problem in preference to full air conditioning.

Lighting

Inappropriate and inadequate lighting is probably the most common reason for people thinking that an older building is unpleasant and unsuitable for modern use. Older buildings can particularly benefit from the use of a well-designed lighting system using all the types of lighting covered in chapter 3.3.7, i.e.

- Ambient lighting
- Accent lighting
- Task lighting
- Decorative lighting
- Kinetic lighting

Parking

Parking provision can be very difficult in older buildings without any current provision. The solutions are a) off site parking, b) negotiating parking with neighbouring owners in return for access across MoJ land, c) using falls across the site to utilise basements for parking, d) acquiring adjacent premises with parking. For city centre sites with good public transport, very little or no parking may be necessary. The need for parking should be challenged. Historic court houses are likely to be retained mainly in major cities, where good public transport obviates the need for parking.

Custody van dock

Access for custody vans is one of the key factors mitigating against continuing use of the building for custody courts. Whilst a choice of access and egress points for custody vans is ideal, a single point will almost always be ultimately acceptable. People in custody must not have to walk in hand cuffs from the van across a public space into the custody area. The vehicle must be able to pull off the road into a van dock (which can be roofed or open) and gates closed to conceal the view of the prisoners. The vehicle should ideally exit forwards in case of trouble, but if this is vital in a certain case but not possible in the space available, the van can turn around during the day to be in the best position for exiting. Solutions to creating a van dock include acquiring adjacent land, utilising the fall on the site to access a basement, closing a side street to the public or accessing from the rear via another owner's service yard.

Custody accommodation

Where custody accommodation is not available or is inadequate the consideration of using the court building for non-custodial cases should be made.

Where the quantity of cell accommodation is too low and there a number of poor quality converted courts it may be possible to reduce the number of courts to match the available custody facility. Standard individual cells can be joined together to create large shared cells for up to 8 people. Form group cells divided up in the past can be reinstated. This can increase capacity considerably. A review of actual local cell requirements may well reduce the allowance from that in the standard automated Schedule of Requirements. In historic buildings, the cells have frequently been updated and changed in the past, so there is rarely much difficulty from a heritage point of view in altering them to meet modern standards. Often affray escape routes are missing in older custody areas. It is sometimes possible to create such a route by excavating or reopening areas of unused basement below historic buildings. Basement often do not extend for the full area of the building above, particularly where there is a fall on the site. A common problem is that the cells are in an adjacent building, usually a police station or town hall, and that building is closing down, leaving the court building without cells. A new build cell block is usually the best solution to a lack of adequate cell accommodation.

Graffiti and vandalism

The solution to graffiti vandalism on all buildings is to avoid blank walls, make access difficult, have no areas hidden from public view, provide colour, texture and detail on all reachable surfaces, have quality finishes, and remove any graffiti as soon as it occurs. On historic buildings, the quality, texture and detail of the finishes is often already there. However, if the building is scruffy or badly maintained it will still encourage vandals since psychologically they will think that if nobody else cares about the building why should they. External floodlighting, particularly uplighting, can discourage close access for graffiti. Railings placed in front of walls (a common traditional detail) can prevent access to the wall for graffiti.

3.1.6 Environmental sustainability

For a court building to be sustainable various criteria have to be incorporated in the design from the start. These are: 1) the use of natural ventilation (avoiding the use of air conditioning), 2) use of windows to achieve natural lighting (minimising artificial lighting), 3) energy conscious design, particularly with regard to transport of materials and the use of craftsman labour rather than off site technological processes 4) waste minimisation including the reuse of existing buildings, and 5) utilisation of the existing natural assets of the site, including ecology, topography, existing landscape planting, prevailing wind, orientation and acoustic screening. Orientation is probably the greatest single factor in creating a low energy building.

The functional elements of the building should be located to exploit all these criteria. Areas requiring quiet and relaxing views should face retained soft landscaping and trees. Areas requiring quiet need to be located in the lea of any existing or proposed acoustic screening formed by existing buildings or the massing of the new building. Office areas should be shallow plan to permit natural lighting. Courtrooms within deep plans should be located on the top floor of the building. All courtrooms must have access to the outside by walls or roof for natural lighting and ventilation. The public should be encouraged to use stairs rather than lifts by locating the stairs prominently in the entrance, and with the lifts tucked away. Topography should be exploited to achieve at-grade entries for different functions and to minimise the use of lifts. Natural water sources should be exploited for water, heating and cooling. Materials should be procured and processed as locally as possible, and ideally recycled from site. (fig 3.37)

Courts, which are built adjacent to noisy railway lines (as at Grenoble (fig 3.38) and Colchester and the proposals for Aylesbury and Gloucester) are designed so that the building forms an acoustic shield to the rest of the building, permitting the use of opening windows elsewhere.

Environmental sustainability is often erroneously considered to be part of the services design and provision. However, the most sustainable buildings theoretically have minimal services. Sustainability therefore must be integral to the basic concept design, not something added on by the services engineer or introduced by a BREEAM assessment.

fig 3.37 Caernarfon reused stone wall

fig 3.38 Grenoble

3.2 Form

3.2.1 Form and massing

The form and massing of the building will be limited by a combination of the site layout restrictions and potential and the internal planning requirements. There are certain internal volumetric and relationship requirements that will have a strong impact on the form and massing of the building, and these will have to be considered at the earliest stage in the design process. Even if there are other functions included in the building (e.g. offices, retail, parking, police station, probation, council facilities) the specific requirements of the courts will have a dominant effect on the building.

The function of the courts requires specific size and layout of courtrooms – see plans and grouping arrangements.

The requirement for natural ventilation and lighting within courtrooms requires a 6m height at the maximum point of the ceiling, together with opening windows at high level. (fig 3.39)

Fig 3.39 Newport, 6m ceiling height to give stack effect natural ventilation

This may be achieved with windows, rooflights or chimneys. Assisted natural ventilation, where air is blown, ducted or chilled at climatic extremes can reduce the height requirements and ease environmental management. This may be particularly appropriate for smaller hearing rooms, County Courts and Tribunals. The natural ventilation requirement also encourages the use of atria to naturally preheat the incoming air in winter, and bring light into the depth of the building.

The height and ventilation requirements of the courtrooms ideally dictate that they are located on the top floor of the building. In buildings with large numbers of courts it tends to dictate complex cross-sections to the building to achieve the natural light and ventilation.

The constantly changing IT requirements of new courtrooms require the provision of raised floors. This affects floor to floor heights.

Smaller court buildings tend to be best planned as two or three storey buildings, due to their complex functional relationships. Those housing 12 or more courts have been found to be most efficient in a linear form with offices over.

There is a requirement for the public to recognise the presence of the law court in the town, as a reflection of the importance of the law in society. This means that the building must have a civic presence, and the law court function must visually dominate any other function within the building.

The public needing to use the building must easily find the entrance and find it welcoming. This includes those with disabilities or small children. The entrance must therefore be obvious, welcoming and at natural pedestrian ground level.

The entrance hall needs to ensure a flow of large numbers of people at the start and end of the day, people trying to find their way around the building, and people using the enquiry desk and cause list. The enquiry desks, lift, stairs and direction to the public waiting areas in the court-halls need to be immediately visible from the main entrance door. Ideally, the court entrances should also be visible from the entrance hall. This tends to encourage a double height entrance hall or the entrance hall in the base of an atrium.

The office functions need to be in adaptable office space, which will be open plan rather than cellular in future. The office areas should, therefore, have a dimension of 6m to 12m from window to core (with 9m preferred), or 15m to 18m from window to window. This precludes deep plans on the office floors. Therefore, office areas need to be on the perimeter of deep plan floor plates or on the top floor with a smaller footprint.

Offices should have opening windows, so need to be located away from areas of noise or air pollution.

The waiting areas for the public, and for child and vulnerable witnesses should, if possible, have windows with pleasant views. This will affect where they can be located, dependent on the site analysis.

Rooms for magistrates and judges should have opening windows with pleasant views, if possible, but must not be overlooked. This often encourages courtyards.

The very limited requirements for car parking can encourage increased site development densities in inner urban sites.

The requirement for natural ventilation significantly reduces the plant room area required over that for air-conditioned buildings.

3.2.2 Building plan forms

The planning of law courts, with their intricate circulation systems for various groups of people who must never meet, except in the courtroom itself, makes law courts one of the most complex building types in existence. Many centuries of experience have highlighted best practice in how to resolve these circulation and daylighting difficulties, but new aspects (such as new technology) lead to new problems and new solutions. Such complexity makes law courts a more difficult building type to design than most. Law courts are probably one of the most challenging building types to design for any architect. When the law courts are combined with other functions, such as offices, a police station or commercial development, the complexity is even more extreme. To make them into a great work of architecture requires the most talented of architects.

The diagrams of room relationships shown here (from the CSDG, Section 3 Functional Relationships), are the keys to the planning of a court building. The dimensions of the layout arrangement of the courtrooms, court hall and judicial areas, with associated facilities for jury, custody, consultation rooms etc are the key to planning any court building.

For initial planning purposes, benchmark areas have been set as a target for the floor area of court buildings. An area for the type of court is given, plus an additional area per courtroom for all other uses, which varies dependant on the number of courts in the building. To achieve the target areas the design will have to be very efficiently planned, with minimal corridors and particularly careful control of the space allocated to plant rooms and storage. An automated Schedule of Requirements (SoR) is available as part of the CSDG and the BIM suite, and gives the definitive areas.

Additional multi-purpose rooms for offices or interview rooms are, however, of considerable benefit to the future flexibility of a court building. Future flexibility and adaptability of layouts to meet changing needs are important to the long-term functionality of the court building.

Studies of typology have shown that a two-storey option is generally preferred for courthouses of up to 12 courts, with double height courtrooms and an office floor over and a custody area below. For the larger court complexes of the future (typically with 36 courtrooms) a linear plan with 2 levels of courtrooms and a custody basement plus rooftop office space is the preferred and most efficient arrangement.

All courtrooms within a building should be on one level where practical.

It is generally the case that multi-storey court arrangements are less economic in both space requirement and in management and running costs.

Four general typological arrangements have been found to work for court buildings.

The Linear Plan

The linear plan is the most basic arrangement and has substantial advantages over other arrangements (fig 3.40).

Its prime characteristic is that courtrooms are sandwiched between the magistrates'/ judicial zone and the courthall/public zone. Both the magistrates'/judicial zone and the courthall/public zone consequently have substantial external wall. For courthouses of up to eight courts, where all courtrooms will be in a single storey, the linear plan enables good daylight and natural ventilation to all three zones. The courthall arrangement allows for clarity of public circulation and maximum visual supervision with the minimum of staff. This arrangement can be double banked with a central courthall and courts either side.

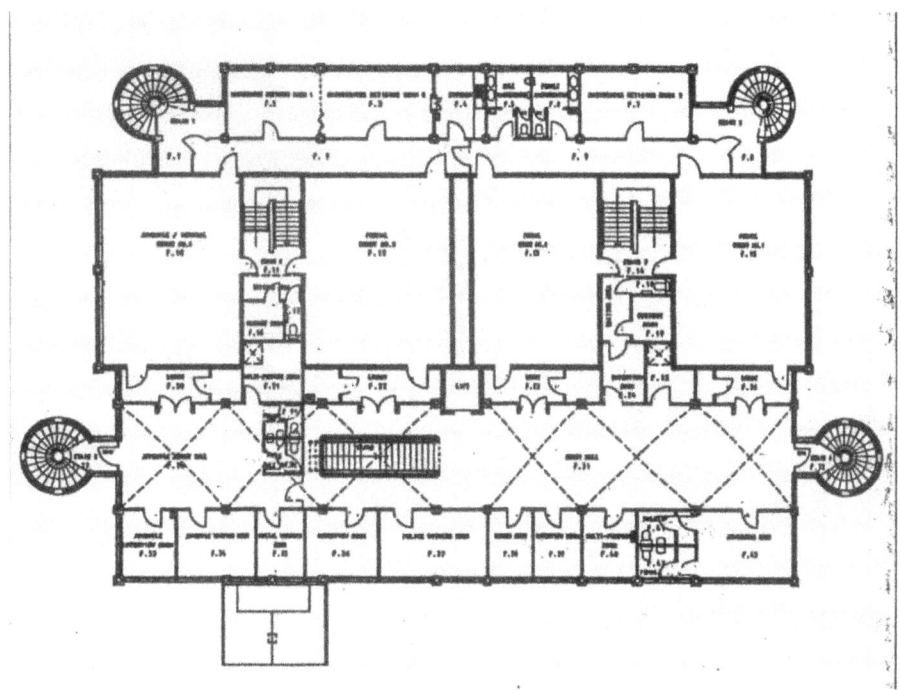

Fig 3.40 Basildon

This arrangement loses its clarity when several storeys of courtroom accommodation are planned. Two levels of courts are the ideal maximum. In particular, it is difficult to daylight the lower courtrooms buried in the centre of the plan. The linear form creates a long, relatively thin building and may not be suitable to all sites: however, sites that can accommodate this form will be favoured. The linear form can be developed to accommodate adult and youth courthalls on one floor with clarity and good supervision of both and the possibility of dual use of at least one court. The linear plan need not be straight, and it may be curved or angled to fit the site.

The Central Courthall

In this arrangement, the courthall serves courtrooms to each side with the magistrates'/ judicial zone being split into two wings. The advantage of this over a linear plan is in the squarer, deeper plan that results which has a relatively smaller surface area to volume, all other things being equal. Again, if arranged on a single storey, courtrooms can be naturally lit and ventilated. The public circulation/courthall area may be most compact in this arrangement: however, the magistrates'/judicial circulation and its link to the administrative zone are more complicated and extended.

The accommodation ancillary to the courthall can be difficult to plan when this typology is adopted. This arrangement can suit a stacked configuration of groupings of four courtrooms per floor where, despite the multi-storey layout, all three zones can be day lit and naturally ventilated.

The Peripheral Courthall

This is the reverse of the central courthall, the magistrates'/judicial zone sits between the courtrooms with two courthalls, one on each side. MoJ does not favour this arrangement. The major disadvantage of this is the confusion generated by having two courthalls on each floor, for the public circulation system, and this may be more onerous in staffing levels to ensure visual supervision. Additionally, the courtrooms on multi-level court arrangements have no access to natural light or natural ventilation. Examples from the 1970s had to be air conditioned and use 50% more energy than assisted natural ventilation courts, which became the norm. Generally, this solution is to be avoided.

Atrium Solutions

These are not variants on the relationships between the principal zones and the external wall, as are the others listed above, but are attempts to clarify public circulation in multi-storeyed buildings. The atrium idea can be applied to each of the types above and they may help with orientation as the public moves around the building. Sometimes the atrium is used to separate the offices from the court suites, particularly where additional offices are included in the scheme, e.g. for ancillary or regional usage. Atrium solutions tend to be the preferred design.

The general policy on environmental considerations is that natural ventilation and lighting are desired in all areas. In practice, solutions have included a range of responses varying from fully sealed air-conditioned buildings to naturally lit and ventilated buildings. It is likely that a "mixed use" response will be required for most sites. There is a strong bias in favour of passive low technology systems being preferred by MoJ; therefore the "mixed use" response should have a dominance of non-mechanical or non-power consuming types of solutions.

Natural ventilation is the preferred option, however sites in areas of high air pollution or suffering from noise pollution may require a special strategy to be deployed.

Courtrooms are particularly noise sensitive. A strategy for dealing with sites that suffer from extraneous noise (traffic, aeroplanes, rail or other sources) should be developed at an early stage by the Design Team. This usually involves careful use of the massing of the building to form a barrier to the noise source.

The sketch model from the CSDG indicates how the diagrammatic planning described above might be turned into a building. The example is a two-storey magistrates' court building with four courts on a generous site, but the logic also works for Crown and County Courts and tight urban sites. Note how the entrance hall and courthall can form an atrium that clarifies and reduces public circulation.

3.2.3 Appearance, Aesthetics and Architecture

For many centuries, it has been accepted that there are three criteria which must be satisfied to achieve good architecture. These have been traditionally called "firmness, commodity and delight", after Vitruvius. Firmness, i.e. build quality, structural soundness, functioning services, watertight roof, etc is a fundamental building requirement. Commodity, i.e. functionality, adequate size, suitable room relationships, useful external spaces, appropriate privacy and acoustic separation, etc, form the brief for any court building and are the core of the CSDG and the BIM models produced by MoJ. Delight, (also known as impact, beauty, pleasantness, aesthetics, etc.) is what turns a merely technically competent building into good architecture with design flare.

In 2002 there was an inter-departmental initiative to improve the quality of public buildings and the spaces that they create under the title of "Better Public Buildings, a proud legacy for the future". The principle was that good design should not only enhance the lives of those who work in or use public buildings, but that design excellence should enhance the wider environment, both physically in the immediate vicinity of the building and also in terms of sustainability. This idealistic aim cannot be faulted, even though nearly twenty years later we are in a very different situation. The "delight" aspect of a court building is best considered under the three aspects of context, form and image. This helps structure the thinking for both the designer and for people assessing the design.

Context

The site and context of the site should, in part, determine the design of the building. Townscape factors such as axial views to the site, the site facing a public square, prominent trees, the site being on the inside or outside curve of a road or the site being viewed prominently due to topography, should all be responded to in the architecture of the building. Appropriate responses might be a symmetrical façade, a prominent entrance feature, a tower, a courtyard, a prominent and characterful skyline, or a grouping of geometric volumes. The specific solution will depend on the internal layout, the site shape and the position of the public entrance.

Local context, both in the immediate and wider vicinity, should also, to a certain extent, be reflected in the materials and detailing of the outside of the building. Using local brick, stone and roof tiles, the colours of the traditional local buildings, the scale of the adjacent buildings and distinctive local design features such as window types, roof styles and skyline features is a common and very appropriate response. However, there are other equally appropriate responses, such as contrasting with the local vernacular (where the vernacular would be inappropriately twee for a law court) or responding to the local desire for an expression of the dynamism and innovation of a regenerating city. The choice of solution should be clear and decisive, not half-hearted and fussy.

The scale of the local environment should influence the massing of the design solution. A typical four-court building might be much more massive than the local buildings when set in the context of a small market town or residential area. It might, therefore, need to be designed as a grouped series of masses or buildings to reduce the scale. Also, expressing the height of the courtrooms within a bold roof shape might reduce the façade height. In contrast, the same size building might seem too puny in the context of a major city centre, and visually emphasising or exaggerating the size, height and mass of the building might be appropriate. In this situation, a single bold geometric mass of building might be appropriate, with the height of the courtrooms or atrium emphasised on the main façade, and the topography used to emphasise the height and dominance from the approach.

A solution for a particularly large building in an intimate context is to select a site that has a relatively small street frontage, but which opens out into a large hidden rear site, as at Cambridge magistrates' court or the Leper Hospital site in Warwick (fig 3.41)

Form

The functional aspects of the form and planning of the building have been discussed above. The aesthetics of plan and massing are something which needs to be considered from the earliest stages in parallel with the functional aspects.

The sequence of major internal spaces should logically lead the public from the main entrance to the courthalls and to the courtrooms, and then back out again. The route should be obvious without the need for signing.

For other functions sought by users, the architectural sequence should lead from the entrance doors to the information desk then to all other facilities along short, clear, well sign-posted, well lit, pleasant routes.

Fig 3.41 Warwick leper hospital, potential court site

Courts are inherently stressful places: this problem should not be exacerbated by people getting lost or not knowing where to go.

The use of natural light along and at the end of a corridor makes the corridor more welcoming and encourages people to use it, if this is desired. This is also helped by corridors of generous width.

Each of the major rooms and spaces should be designed as a clear, simple, well-proportioned volume.

Rooms should be a simple geometric space, usually rectangular.

Certain larger spaces can be architecturally a group of two or three simple linked geometric spaces. In that case, each geometric volume needs to be expressed architecturally, e.g. as an apse or bay in a courtroom or entrance hall, or as an enfilade of rooms for waiting areas and open-plan offices. Where rooms in an enfilade are not fully separated, windows, columns or architectural features on the walls or ceiling should be used to define the rooms.

In very large volumes a smaller room can be expressed within the larger volume, e.g. as a pod or balcony in an atrium.

In very large volumes, particularly glazed atria, the geometry of the space can be derived from the space between two larger geometric solid volumes, where effectively an external courtyard or street is glazed over. (fig 3.42)

Rooms should not be amorphous, leftover spaces. They should not be randomly L-shaped, nibbled away at the corners to create other rooms, or have arbitrary or asymmetric angles.

Fig 3.42 Southampton magistrates' court

Rooms should be designed as volumes, not just plan areas. The height of the room and the geometry of any exposed roof structure, dome, vault or other modelled ceiling should be considered. This is particularly important where a generous ceiling height is needed for natural ventilation and in corridors.

The main entrance and entrance hall require a civic presence to reflect the status of the Law in society, and engender respect for the decisions made in the courts. This can be achieved by being the focus of the townscape, through symmetry and formality in the architecture, through a generous use of space and height internally and using steps to the entrance (though allowing at-grade or ramped access too). There should also be a generous external gathering space outside the entrance. The main entrance should symbolically be the image of the court, and the place outside which the Press photograph those seeking publicity after a case.

All windows should be positioned to maximise the quantity and quality of both light and views.

Windows on only one side of a room will tend to give glare. This can be eased by having light coloured reveals and astragals. Alternatively, further smaller windows on the opposite side of the room or in the ceiling can balance the glare.

The position of the windows, their shape and any mullions should be used to frame the best view available. Views generally consist of foreground, middle ground and distance, which due to perspective tend to be at low level, straight ahead and at high level respectively. Windows should therefore be of vertical proportions, and the sill should be below table level for the room. In larger rooms the sill should be at floor level to maximise views from all parts of the room. The window head should be as high as possible to maximise both the view of the sky and the light penetration into the room.

Courtrooms should only have a sky or landscape view, to avoid the distractions of people and traffic.

In open plan offices and waiting areas the room should be designed and adaptable furniture layouts proposed where the maximum of users can benefit from the view.

Doors should be visually expressed as a hierarchy, so that where there are many doors, e.g. in a courthall or corridor, rooms such as the courtrooms can be clearly identified architecturally from interview rooms or cupboards.

Image

Law courts, to a greater extent than almost any other building type, have a symbolic function in their architecture. Court buildings need to be seen to be there and seen to be public, authoritative and important in society, whether an individual has reason to use them or not. Unlike our other buildings, therefore, court buildings cannot be hidden away on an industrial estate or be anonymous suburban office buildings, nor can they be seen to be high security compounds or visually oppressive.

A new court is a public building and should be recognisable as such. It should contribute to its location, wherever it is sited. It should function well, be clearly organised, be approachable and represent the ideas of equality before the law, stability and permanence.

Attending court can be an intimidating experience. The building should counter that by putting users at their ease. It must be remembered that members of the public do not visit courts regularly. It will be the first time for many and some will be apprehensive and anxious, so the building must be legible, making it easy for people to find their way around without needing to rely heavily on signage. Good design will produce a building that caters for all users. The needs of disabled and mobility impaired users must be fully considered from the beginning of the design process, so that all people can move around the building by the same routes, without the need for awkward and visually intrusive special measures.

A building with graffiti and vandalism is also intimidating to many users, particularly witnesses, victims and jurors. The materials and details of the building both internally and externally must be designed to discourage graffiti and vandalism and ease its speedy removal. High quality materials with plenty of modelling, craftsmanship and texture tend to discourage vandalism, as do practical traditional details such as railings or plants in front of blank ground floor walls to keep people at a distance. Areas that encourage external loitering also tend to attract graffiti and can seem intimidating.

There is a concern about the public's perception of judicial independence, and courts being too closely associated with the prosecution. Where the Police and CPS or even prisons are sharing a building with courts it is important that, at the main entrance the courts in the building visually predominate.

The ideal way of expressing any court building as symbolically a court is for the courtrooms themselves to be expressed visually as the key element in the design. This can be in the external form, the facades or the roofline. This ought to be a key requirement of any court building.

The image or aesthetics of a building are often thought to be solely about the external appearance, e.g. classical proportions and the Golden Section. This is a very simplistic view, and historically inaccurate. Aesthetics builds on the past and changes direction when an approach becomes too extreme. An understanding of changes in aesthetics helps not only the design of new buildings but in particular it also helps when working with old buildings.

- The classical architecture of ancient Greece, Rome and the Far East, and their revivals, relied on simple mathematical proportions of the principal elements of a façade and plan to give beauty. The entire building was one symmetrical unit, with the plan divided up internally into a series of axially linked volumes. All decoration had to be based on historical precedent.

- With the Baroque designs of the 18th to early 20th century people realised that something more was needed, and the idea of awe or drama was added, where, for instance, as you walk through a small tight dark space you would suddenly emerge into something huge, dramatic and brightly lit. Architecture was treated as theatre, to instil emotions in users and express power and the hierarchy of society.

- From the late 19th century onwards the ideas of the Arts and Crafts Movement developed out of the Gothic revival and came to dominate thinking. The various parts of a building should be orientated functionally (to maximise views, sunlight, access etc) rather than formally and axially, and that craftsmanship mattered more than a conspicuous show of wealth.

- This led on to the modern movement of the mid-20th century where total freedom of plan was normal, innovative materials were encouraged, machine-like qualities were valued and the quality of light dominated design.

- In the late 20th century the excesses of modernism (short life, high energy usage, disorientating planning, brutal materials) were tempered by the influence of post-modernism to give more user-friendly buildings related to their environment and context.

- Current thinking in architecture is a distillation of all of these. Architecture now requires logical planning, obvious entrances, simple use of sustainable natural quality materials, low energy usage, long-life buildings, a concern for the context, appearance reflecting the function, maximisation of views and orientation, concern for the environment and a pleasant, interesting place in which to work. Grabbing some drama from the context or brief is also high on the agenda. In addition to this it ought also to be beautiful. This is the aesthetic aim of court buildings, if not all good architecture.

A new court building should be an imaginative and appropriate response to the local urban or rural area and come to be seen as an asset to its surroundings. It must provide a good internal environment, with high quality natural lighting to all the principal spaces, especially the public waiting areas and courtrooms. It must provide a comfortable, controlled environment, which is neither too hot nor too cold at all times of the year and working day.

Building design – architecture – is an applied art. Of course, the designer must meet the functional and constructional requirements; the scheme design must satisfy the client's brief. However, a good design will go well beyond this, orchestrating these demands into a legible, coherent, imaginative whole that is pleasing to the eye and mind. A court building is an important public building, a symbol of the judicial system. The public associate court buildings with civic architecture of a high standard; over 20% of courts are housed in listed buildings. New courts should live up to the expectations raised by this association, but this does not mean they should be pompous or overbearing.

The design excellence required for court buildings must provide much more than the mere functional needs of the client. It must create an environment that delights and excites the senses and stretches the imagination.

3.2.4 EXTERNAL SPACES

MoJ worked with CABE (The Commission for Architecture and the Built Environment) to encourage good urban design, to develop a policy to ensure that public buildings contribute to the public realm. CABE may now have shrunk and been subsumed into the Design Council, but the principles they developed are sound and live on. A new building should achieve seven principles of urban design.

- Character – to create a place that strengthens or even creates for the first time that sense of unique identity.
- Continuity and enclosure – to create spaces between buildings that can be as important to the public as the buildings themselves, with a clear distinction between public and private space.
- Public realm – to achieve a quality streetscape with attention to detailed design.
- Ease of movement – to strengthen the urban structure by adding a clear network of connected spaces and routes.
- Legibility – to use landmarks, gateways, focal points, vistas and visual links to help people find their way.
- Diversity – to mix uses so as to create a continuity of activity throughout the day.
- Adaptability – to make the development adaptable enough to be able to respond to changing social, technological and economic conditions over time.

This approach is exemplified in such schemes as Bristol Civil Justice Centre, Derby Magistrates' court, Westminster magistrates' court, and the historic Salford courts (fig 3.43) where the form of the building is primarily subservient to the external space it creates.

Fig 3.43 Salford

3.2.5 Major internal spaces

3.2.5.1 Entrances

The main entrance is the transition between the external environment and the internal spaces of the court building. For many people, it is the first introduction to the functioning of the law.

As stated earlier, the main entrance requires a civic presence to reflect the status of the Law in society, and engender respect for the decisions made in the courts. This can be achieved by being the focus of the townscape, as at Preston Crown, the Supreme Court and Wolverhampton Crown, through symmetry and formality in the architecture, and through a generous use of space and height internally, as at Newport and Wolverhampton (3.44).

Fig 3.44 Wolverhampton Crown Court

This should continue within the internal space. The main entrance should symbolically be the image of the court, and the place outside which the Press photograph those seeking publicity after a case. There needs to be space to exit and meet the press without blocking the entry by others to the building, or the exit by others from the building. The entrance to Bristol magistrates' court leads the eye to the entrance through the use of dramatic acute angled architecture and careful lighting. The Supreme Court uses the historic architecture enhanced by symmetrical modern landscaping and the careful removal of a tree to reveal and dramatise the entrance from Parliament Square. Leamington Spa combined court uses a dramatic sweep of stairs and ramps leading users up to the glazed entrance between two more solid blocks of building, so that the entrance is obvious from the classical terraces of the spa town and from the botanical gardens opposite.

The main entrance should be entered via a draught lobby and security point. From the entry point the courthall, stairs, lift, public enquiry counter and payments desk should be visible. This sums up the fundamental requirements of the entry to a court building. Westminster magistrates' court is a clear expression of this requirement.

The security point varies with the size and risk stature of the building, but in principle consists of a security table with a security guard and a metal detecting arch. There needs to be space before the security point for people entering to queue in the dry and space after for people to retrieve their possessions and put them away before finding out where to go. With higher security buildings, the table is replaced with a scanner, and there can be multiple arches. There needs to be somewhere to store the knives, guns, syringes drugs and cameras confiscated or held by the security staff. The area is very busy at the start of the day and for returning after lunch. When people exit, they do not pass through security, but usually use a side door adjacent to the bank of security entrances.

Discrete interview rooms should be accessible off the entrance, adjacent to the enquiry counter. The public enquiry counter/ information point must be located within or opening onto the entrance hall. Where county courts are co-located with magistrates' courts the public users for a) county court and magistrates' court family jurisdiction and b) magistrates' court criminal and civil jurisdiction should be directed to their separate circulation routes from the entrance hall after passing through security. Separate entrances to the building for the two groups may be appropriate where particular circumstances dictate. The circumstances in which separate entrances to the building might be appropriate for these parties or for youth courts would be: a) where the building is particularly large; or b) where there is an existing building with two entrances and it would not be viable to alter the building to achieve one entrance and security point. Separate entrances are not required where county civil and family and magistrates' family sit on separate days from magistrates' criminal. Separate obvious and labelled entrances for witnesses are not encouraged, since these form a security risk for the witnesses. Secure or sensitive witnesses are generally instructed to use discrete staff entrances or a discrete unmarked entrance on an elevation out of sight of the main entrance.

3.2.5.2 Court Hall

The courthall is the principal waiting and circulation area of the courthouse. It should lead directly from the entrance area, and may well function as part of the entrance hall. Depending on the design and size of the building it may be on the ground floor, on the first floor or there may be multiple courthalls on different floor levels. In the latter situation, it is usually preferable to have the multiple courthalls forming balconies open to a greater atrium space, so that the entire layout of the building is immediately visible on entry. Manchester Civil Justice Centre achieves this particularly well, as does Manchester magistrates' court and Preston crown court, though in very different ways.

The main function of the courthall is to offer direct access to all courtrooms on a particular floor (via lobbies) and to a number of ancillary areas.

The courthall planned is best planned as a simple rectangular space which has the advantage of easily understood circulation and wayfinding without signposting. (fig 3.45)

Courthalls, which are irregular in shape, with islands of accommodation within the total space, can produce confused circulation and may result in difficult communication and control. Simple forms with clear sight lines to all parts reduce vandalism. Chair groupings, plants and the architecture of the room should be used to break up space to encourage small groupings of people but not to interrupt overall sight lines through the space.

When a court is in session the courthall will be under supervision from an usher. Means may need to be provided to restrict or discourage access to the courthall when the courtrooms are not in session during office hours, whilst leaving the main public entrance and reception open to allow access to the public counter.

The courthall in magistrates' courts should be physically and visually divided between adult and youth court areas. The simplest solution is to have the courts on different floors, where this is possible. These may share a common entrance hall and entrance from the street. To maximise flexibility in the use of courts, adult and youth courthalls may be arranged on the same level and connected with lockable doors to enable both courthalls and all courtrooms to be used for adult cases when the youth courts are not in session and vice versa. A separate youth entrance to the youth side of the courthall will need to be provided to prevent either adults or youths having to pass each other. Where a youth courthall is permanently set aside for youth session, there is an advantage to be gained in locating the advocates' and the Crown Prosecution Service accommodation between the main courthall and the youth courthall, with a dedicated entrance to a common lobby linking the two halls. This gives advocates access to both areas, while maintaining the necessary segregation in respect of other court users. Flexibility in use is very important. Some courts choose to hold youth sessions on only certain days of the week. This is a very practical and efficient arrangement for smaller court buildings. Others prefer to have dedicated youth courtrooms. This can change over time, as can the relative quantities of each type of case. The design of the courthall should allow for both short term and long term changes.

Fig 3.45 Westminster

Persons attending family courts find it extremely unpleasant to be obliged to be in the same area as those attending criminal courts. Separate areas within the courthall should be allocated for the purpose where family courts and criminal courts are in the same building. In particular, family and youth courts should not share the same waiting space, unless the cases are listed on different days. The reason for this is that defendants in criminal courts, and their associates, tend to be accused of, or have committed, crimes. There is no suggestion of any criminality in civil or family courts – there is no right and wrong party, just an equitable, fair but final decision. Families do not want their children to have to associate with criminals, nor to perceive that one of their parents has done something wrong.

Where county courts are co-located with magistrates' courts the public users must be separated into a) county court users and magistrates' court family jurisdiction users and b) magistrates' court criminal (including youth) jurisdiction users and magistrates' court civil jurisdiction users. They must have separate courthalls. Where the courthalls are at a different level or are remote from the entrance hall the routes from the entrance to courthall should also be separate. Where usage of courtrooms is shared at different times, the defendants and public from the criminal jurisdiction must not pass through the courthall of the civil and family jurisdiction, when it is in use, to access the courtrooms.

The principal purpose of the courthall is to wait for attendance in a court case. This can be very stressful for all parties – defendants, their friends and family, the witnesses and the victims. The reduction of stress is the key design aim for the courthall.

The way to reduce stress is to design a space that is calming and that has the potential to distract the mind of those waiting onto something else. The space should be light and airy. Views out are important – ideally to a park or trees or a river, though anywhere with activity such as a street or square or roofscape is suitably calming and distracting. (fig 3.46)

Fig 3.46 Belfast Laganside courthall

Belfast Laganside courts, Huntingdon magistrates' court, City of Westminster magistrates' court, Manchester Civil Justice Centre, Manchester magistrates' court and Leamington Spa Justice Centre are excellent examples.

In a courthouse, people may be required to wait for long periods of time and it is usually inconvenient for them to leave the building. There are therefore other functions ancillary to the courthall which should be within or accessed off the courthall. Toilets are the most obvious, as are basic refreshment facilities serving the courthall. Refreshments should be sited to serve both the adult and youth courthall in magistrates' courts, whilst maintaining the necessary visual separation between the two. Staffed provision is only considered in the largest of court buildings, a dispensing machine, providing hot and cold drinks must be provided, and dispensing machines for hot and cold food are necessary if the building is located where there are no nearby catering facilities. Dispensing machines may also be a useful means of providing refreshments for the witnesses' waiting room or rooms. Where court buildings are developed as part of a larger complex, the provision of commercial cafes adjacent to the courts are very much to be encouraged. They have the convenience of in house facilities, but are more commercially viable and enable different parties to eat in different locations.

A room may be required, particularly in family courts, for the use of mothers or fathers with young children, providing an area for feeding and/or changing a baby without disturbing occupants of the courthall. It should include a sink and WC. Since either parent could be changing the baby or escorting the child to the toilet, this should not be part of the male or female toilets. Whilst breast feeding is becoming an acceptable practice in public, in a court building where there may be people accused of sexual offences in the courthall, there should be provision for breast feeding in privacy off the courthall.

Youths or children not accompanied by a parent or other responsible adult may need supervision in the courthall, either in open waiting space, in closed rooms, or in a secure space if they are unruly. The planning of this accommodation should be geared to the maximum use of waiting / consultation rooms, rather than the provision of separate suites for all these categories. Youths must not be allowed to terrorise or intimidate other court users.

3.2.5.3 Courtrooms

The courtroom is the focal point of the courthouse, the place where all parties in a case will meet for the first time. The plan of the courtroom must incorporate specific and well-defined relationships between the various participants by means of carefully arranged sight-lines, distances and levels.

The courtroom occupies a position between the public side and the restricted side of building. On the public side, access is by way of sound lobbies from the courthall. Separate Judge's and Jurors' restricted circulation lead to the Judge's entrance to the bench and into the jury waiting room respectively. Access to the Courtroom for Jurors is from the jury waiting room, and for witnesses from the witnesses' waiting room, or the public concourse. Direct secure access is provided from the custody area via the defendants' waiting area into the dock.

Segregated circulation routes are provided so that the judge or magistrates, jury, and defendant(s) (if in custody) and ideally witnesses, can make their way to the court without meeting each other or any other users (eg members of the public). The degree of separation depends on the type of court. In a Crown court, all parties are strictly separated. In a simple tribunal hearing room the judge or tribunal chairman only has an emergency escape route, but otherwise all parties use the same corridor and entrance. Juries can share corridors with magistrates/judges since juries are always escorted thus avoiding the risk if influence. Witnesses must not share corridors with juries or magistrates/judges, due to risk of intimidation, influence or violence.

Within the courtroom dedicated entrances are provided for (a) judge/magistrates, (b) jury, (c) defendants, (d) public and (e) witnesses. Witnesses can enter via a waiting room outside the courtroom adjacent to the witness box. Neither public nor witnesses pass areas dedicated to other participants (e.g. jury or defendants) on entering or leaving the courtroom. Sensitive witnesses must be able to enter the waiting room without passing through public areas.

The judge must have a clear view of all parts of the courtroom – the defendants, the advocates, the witness, the public and the jury. In particular, the judge must have a clear and equal view of each juror, and as far as possible be able to see what he or she is doing – eg reading documentary evidence or writing notes. Ideally the work surfaces in the jury box should be visible to the judge, but if upstands are installed in front of the work surfaces, the top edges of those upstands should be visible to the judge along their whole length.

Jurors, counsel, witnesses and defendant(s) must be able to see (a) one another, (b) the judge and (c) the jury. The key point is that the jurors (where present) and the judge/magistrates have to see and hear the witnesses and defendants clearly to assess which party (if any) is lying.

The public are to have a general view of the proceedings, but with the minimum possible direct eye contact with the jury in order to reduce the risk of intimidation of jurors.

Court proceedings must be audible to all participants. Witnesses or other parties may require sound amplification.

The minimum dimensions of the courtroom are dictated by the necessary size of furniture and the ergonomic requirements to use and move around the court. The area for benches/chairs etc in the well of the court is intended to allow for a flexible layout, but the disposition of furniture must always leave a passageway both for normal movement within the courtroom, for disabled access, for escape purposes in case of fire, and for escape in case of violence within the court. Court rooms need not be rectangular. There are circular and hexagonal examples in Exeter Cambridge and Warwick.

Access from the courtroom to the judge's side of the bench is restricted to one gate located at the end of the bench furthest from the judge's door. The other end of the bench is enclosed by bench-high panelling spanning from bench to wall. The purpose of this is to enable the judge or magistrates to escape from the courtroom when the defendant or other parties attempt to assault the bench via the steps and gate.

To achieve the requirement for naturally ventilated courtrooms the ceiling height at the highest part of the courtrooms will need to be a minimum of 6m.

Whether a courtroom is used for a Magistrates', Crown or County Court there are elements of furniture etc. within the design that are functionally similar or identical. They include: judges'/magistrates' bench, clerk's desk, witness box, jury desk, press desk, exhibits table, advocates' bench, secure dock, and natural ventilation of courtrooms. These elements can be assembled with adequate spacing and sight lines to design courtrooms in any shape of room. These elements can also be used to design a courtroom in an existing room or older building. The numbers of people accommodated may vary when the court is assembled from these elements. Standardised numbers of seats and precise layouts are no longer dictated, and tend to vary to suit local requirements. In the future, furniture may be designed and built in-house by the prison service.

The dimensions of the advocates' desks are critical to the size of the room. The 850mm desk length means that the benches can be universal for any court. It will take 2 sheets of A4 plus a flat screen computer monitor. (Or 1 sheet of A4 plus a laptop computer and a monitor screen) This must be the size for the first row of advocates' desks. In special circumstances (notably in historic buildings) it may

be possible to reduce the desk size, particularly in the rows behind the front row. A 600mm desk would take 2 sheets of A4 with a screen to the side. A 450mm desk would take one sheet of A4 plus a screen. 850mm is needed for large and long cases with copious paperwork and many advocates (particularly the largest courts and commercial courts). 600mm would be acceptable if advocates shared a screen or if all the seats were not used. 450mm would only be acceptable for quick cases with little paperwork.

In the design of a secure dock visibility through the thick frameless glass of a secure dock is always a crucial factor, particularly where it is constructed within an existing courtroom so that the sight lines are pre-determined. The width of the visible edge of the glass will be important. The glass is used is 18mm to 20mm thick, "water white" glass with non-reflective finish and polished edges, laminated 3 or 4 ply to achieve appropriate integrity and robustness. The design approach is that the security glazing to the dock creates the minimum visual impact within the court. This is primarily to ensure sight lines are not impeded and that there is no cage like oppressive environment for the defendants. Ideally the glass goes from floor to ceiling. In magistrates courts this is often achieved by recessing the dock into the side wall of the court, as at Derby. The standard or non-secure dock is used where there is no particular threat of violence or escape from the defendant. The well at the front of the dock is to discourage vaulting over the dock wall. They are now rarely built in new court buildings.

Natural ventilation or assisted natural ventilation, together with natural lighting, is a requirement in all courtrooms. The implications of this go beyond the mechanical and electrical services aspects of the building and affect the form, planning and massing of the overall building. The height and cross section of the courtroom will need to be designed to allow the air to circulate and ventilate by the stack effect. Opening windows will be required to give cross ventilation. Windows will be required to open directly to the outside or obtain borrowed light over corridors. The extent of the assistance to the natural ventilation (eg fan-assisted air extract or supply, seasonal cooling or heating at extremes of weather) should be kept to the practical minimum, both in terms of plant installed and period in which it needs to be run. The extent of the assistance to the natural ventilation is likely to increase where buildings are being converted from other uses (eg offices converted to County Courts), but the implications of natural ventilation and lighting should be considered when selecting such buildings for conversion. Opening windows in a courtroom is the minimum acceptable standard for buildings converted from other uses. Some of the best examples of courtrooms led by the need for natural light and ventilation are Lincoln magistrates' court, Bournemouth magistrates' court, Truro Crown court and Northampton.

As the changes in level within a court room gradually reduced after 2000, and witnesses have tended to sit to give evidence, rather than stand the sightlines to the witness, particularly from the jury, have become critical in the design of court rooms. Key sightline factors are whether the witness box or table is on a dais, whether the witness is in a wheelchair, the position of the clerk's desk and the position of IT equipment on the clerk's desk. When designing a new or altered courtroom the sightlines to the witness from all parties need to be checked at an early stage to ensure they are suitable.

One of the common challenges in designing a courtroom is how to design a window for borrowed light behind the judges' bench over the judges' corridor. The solutions at Newcastle Quayside crown court (fig 3.47) and Miami Dade courthouse (fig 3.48) are particularly notable.

Fig 3.47 Newcastle

Fig 3.48 Miami Dade courthouse

3.2.5.4 Circulation spaces

The public areas – entrance, courthall and circulation - form the central core or axis from which most non-judicial functions of the Court building radiate. All court users (with the exception of the judiciary and defendants in custody) enter the building by the main entrance door where adequate facilities and space for security checks are provided. The arrival concourse contains the Information/Enquiry Point and the Cause List Display, both of which should be clearly seen on entering the building, as should a 'directions' indicator board. Public circulation then leads to Court Waiting Areas which may be combined with associated circulation to form concourses off which are located courtrooms and the consultation/waiting rooms. Waiting areas and circulation should be visually interesting, preferably with external views.

Public circulation gives direct access to private and semi private accommodation occupied by court staff and staff attached to associated bodies such as Probation as well as custody visits. Access must also be provided to public counters, which form the interface between the public and office staff. Direct access from the arrivals concourse to the Jury Assembly Area and to sensitive witness areas is required. Public toilets appropriately sized are to be provided in locations convenient for Court Waiting/Concourse, normally on each floor. Adequate facilities must be provided for the admission of wheelchairs and handicapped persons and for their subsequent circulation within the building.

The ideal in designing corridors and other circulation spaces is the achievement of short, clear, well sign-posted, well lit, pleasant routes. Light at the end of a corridor, either a window or artificial lighting attracts people to walk down the corridor. The corollary is that a corridor that ends in darkness is somewhere that people will be very reluctant to go. The design of corridors and other aspects of circulation is similar to townscape – people will be encouraged to go where they can see what the route leads to, and to where the route appears to open out into a space that is apparently larger and more important.

When people are familiar with the building, e.g. on the secure side judicial and staff corridors, the pleasantness of the circulation is greatly enhanced by plentiful windows and pleasant views. Natural lighting from one side creates an apparently wider and more relaxing corridor.

On the public side, the ideal is to remove the need for any corridors, with all circulation directly off the entrance hall and courthall. With larger buildings, the judicial circulation tends to increase exponentially, as does the custody circulation. The length of corridors can be reduced by stacking the courts into multi storey buildings. However, this increases the extent of vertical circulation (lifts and stairs), which is more expensive in both capital and running costs.

3.2.5.5 Retiring rooms

Retiring rooms are needed for judges, magistrates, tribunals and juries. Each room has a slightly different function, therefore a different design and size.

The judicial accommodation is located in a secure area of the building with restricted points of access and circulation. The Judiciary will normally arrive at the Court building and enter through restricted entry directly into their own secure circulation off which are located the Judges/Magistrates Retiring Rooms and all areas devoted to Judicial use. Tribunal members often enter the building via the front entrance before entering the judicial area. Other than the Judiciary the only users of the secure circulation in 'working hours' will be staff, i.e. ushers, Court Clerks, security staff and invitees i.e. legal representatives, guests and some members of the public invited to a Judges Room. Invitees will always be escorted and access for all will be either via the Judges/Magistrates entrance of the courtroom or through Staff areas. All entrances will be via a self-locking, secure door. Circulation for Jurors has traditionally been provided separate from judicial circulation. However, since jurors are always supervised by a jury bailiff, the risk of jury contamination is now considered negligible, and jurors can share circulation with the judiciary.

A judge's retiring room is used as a private study for preparation and deliberation on cases. They are also used for meetings with justices / counsel / clerk or other invitees. Up to half of every day may be spent in the retiring room. There is usually a large quantity of shelving to accommodate the judges' legal reference books and his case files. They usually require a toilet for the private use of the judge, since he needs to robe and disrobe. Access is via judges' restricted circulation. Ideally the retiring suite and courtroom will be adjacent. Aural and visual privacy to the Retiring Room is essential. Natural lighting and ventilation by opening windows is necessary. Traditionally the judges' retiring rooms have become a home-from-home with a great deal of personal items. Rooms with character are particularly desirable. Modern offices however are becoming the norm. Some of the best judges' retiring rooms are found in older buildings, particularly where spaces have been converted, particularly attics. The Royal Courts of Justice and the Supreme Court (fig 3.49) have good examples.

Fig 3.49 Supreme Court

In the future open plan shared retiring rooms may be used with private study carrels for individual judges, plus shared meeting rooms.

A magistrates' retiring room is used by a bench of 3 persons who would retire from the courtroom and require a room to briefly discuss the case and agree the verdict and sentence. On infrequent occasions a large room might be shared. Each suite is related to 1 or 2 Courtrooms and the link to the Bench should be as direct as possible via restricted circulation. Ideally the Retiring Suite and Courtroom will be adjacent.

Retiring rooms should be sited in the same storey as the court served and close to the door to the Bench.

There was traditionally one for every two courts, but one per court is becoming more frequent, particularly where large numbers of shorter cases are common, which is increasingly the case. Occasionally in smaller court buildings one in every three retiring rooms is a large retiring room, able to accommodate two or more groups discussing cases simultaneously. Such large retiring rooms double up as a magistrates' assembly area, perhaps with sliding partitions to create even larger areas. As with judges' retiring rooms, aural and visual privacy to the retiring room is essential. Natural lighting and ventilation by opening windows is preferred, but not vital since the rooms are only in use for about 15 minutes at a time. These retiring rooms are not used as offices by the magistrates. The larger retiring rooms and the magistrates' assembly areas are used by magistrates to prepare and process their cases and also used for their office work whilst magistrates are waiting before of after their voluntary duty on the bench.

In tribunals, there are two different types of retiring room. Tribunals require one retiring room per hearing room. Due to the numbers and different parties in the hearing room, it is the tribunal panel that exits the hearing room to a retiring room to deliberate. Ideally retiring rooms should be located close to hearing rooms but not necessarily identified with a particular hearing room (i.e. not having access directly from the hearing room). Hearing rooms will be used for different jurisdictions, including family and civil cases formerly held in County Courts or magistrates' courts with family jurisdiction. but sufficient retiring rooms need to be provided so as not to constrain the number of simultaneous cases taking place at any one time. Usually the retiring room doubles as an emergency escape route for the tribunal panel in the case of a disturbance in the hearing room. The retiring room therefore should be immediately adjacent to the hearing room with the door adjacent to where the panel sits. Ideally there should be another escape door from the retiring room into the corridor or another hearing room. Both doors need to be lockable.

Any civil/family/tribunal resident judiciary or tribunal chairperson will have their own retiring room, office or chambers, which should be located away from the public areas in the venue. In addition, there should be office space for visiting judiciary. Panel members do not have separate retiring rooms or offices. They use the general office space or judicial library If they need to work privately, read the appeal papers or deliberate the appeal.

Jury retiring rooms are for the jury of 12 jurors to retire to whilst considering their verdict or waiting when sent out by the judge for procedural reasons. Empanelled jurors must have no unsupervised contact with anyone other than the Jury Bailiff. Two en-suite toilets are required together with a tea point for the jury bailiff to supply food and drink. They are often located in more remote locations within the building. In many historic buildings, such as the Old Bailey (Central Criminal Court) the jury retiring rooms are located in a mezzanine over the judges retiring rooms to the rear of the courtrooms, utilising the double height of the courtrooms. This is a solution often emulated in new buildings. The room should be as square a shape as possible to accommodate a square or circular table arrangement together with appropriate circulation space. There should be no obvious hierarchy to the table that might indicate that one seat is the chairperson of the jury. Aural and visual privacy is essential. Opening windows for daylight and external reference are vital but they should avoid glare and distractions

3.2.5.6 Consultation rooms

All court buildings function by having a myriad of small consultation and interview rooms which are constantly in use for a few minutes at a time as different parties meet together to agree what can and cannot be said and how to present the latest twist in the case. Some discussions can take place in a huddle in the court hall but most meetings need to have privacy so that advocates do not to reveal their hand to the opposition, or so that they can persuade the clients to reveal for their own good something that they would prefer to hold back.

Multi purpose rooms also known as consultation /waiting rooms or meeting/interview rooms suitable for 2 to 4 people (about 10m^2) need to be provided off the courthall, where advocates and probation officers can interview their clients, or where apprehensive witnesses (or others requiring or desiring privacy) can wait, away from the public areas. There should be 1 or 2 per court room, but in recent years the demand has grown since it has been found that court cases are very much quicker if parties do not have to wait to get the use of a consultation room when the court briefly adjourns.

The function is not only to enable advocates to consult with clients and witnesses in aural and visual privacy, but also to provide a waiting space to give privacy to witnesses and victims whilst waiting to appear in court. They should be informal rooms giving aural and visual privacy without a 'closed in' environment. Natural light should be provided where possible and some visual interest is desirable for stressed people waiting in the rooms.

They should be distributed approximately equally throughout court waiting areas (courthall) and convenient to Courtrooms. They are often located in a bank backing onto the courtroom, and aligning with the courtroom lobby to add additional sound separation to the courtroom. Access must be from the Courthall or its contiguous circulation but NOT from Court sound lobbies.

The peak use of consultation rooms is at the start of the day just before the courts sit, but they are in use throughout the day. Towards the end of the day, as cases finish for the day, their use declines. However, the end of the day is the peak usage for probation, social workers and discussions over fine payment. It is therefore efficient to have consultation rooms shared by all users, rather than having dedicated consultation rooms for specific functions.

Good examples are at Lincoln magistrates' court (fig 3.50), where the consultation rooms are characterful glazed lean-tos within the greater barn like space of the courthall, and Manchester Civil Justice Centre, where the consultation rooms are pods suspended at various dizzying heights within the atrium.

Fig 3.50 Lincoln

3.2.5.7 Offices

On 31st March 2008, the Office of Government Commerce (OGC) issued a report called "Efficiency Standards for Office Space". From 1st April 2008, all Government Departments were required to strive to comply with the space standards in that document. A standard "best practice target" of 10sq.m. per person (of nett internal area) had to be provided. This was derived from a space of 12 sq.m. per workstation at an occupancy rate of 1.2 people per workstation. Subsequently this has been modified to give 10 sq.m. per workstation with 8 or sometimes 7 workstations per 10 people. In HQ buildings, this is now being further reduced to 5 workstations per 10 people, and this is likely to be the target for offices within court buildings.

Despite the reduction in space, and consequent removal of individual offices in favour of open plan offices, all office spaces within support buildings must have the following features that make it a good place in which to work:

- A layout that is open, clear and easy to understand
- A layout that promotes easy communication and accessibility
- Space planning that is intuitive to understand and use
- Diverse working and resting areas
- Areas that make optimum use of the space

- Staff accommodation located in prime areas
- Secondary spaces used for shared facilities e.g. copy areas, storage and breakout should be located centrally.
- A good functional quality of environment, with well-considered lighting, heating and ventilation
- Desking located near to natural light where possible
- Easily accessible breakout areas
- A layout where circulation is clearly defined
- Desking to be located away from main circulation routes and to be protected from corridor space
- Good environmental control
- Natural lighting and ventilation to be available to those who occupy the perimeter space. (This zone is up to 7.5 meters away from the windows or 2 to 2.5 times the floor to ceiling height of the room. This depends on the size and location of the windows, where they are smaller so these dimensions decrease. Comfort in the space, which is not within the perimeter zone, will need to be maintained using artificial light and ventilation thereby effecting the consumption of energy.)

With regard to the efficiency of floor plate – i.e. its size and shape, there is often a misconception that a simple rectangular floor plate is the most efficient shape for an office. It is the most efficient for the developer, but not for the user. The simple rectangular shape **minimises** the proportion of facade to floor area, which is economical to build for the developer, but the user needs to **maximise** the proportion of facade to floor area to enable the maximum number of people to be within a close proximity to a window, and to avoid unusable areas deep within a floor plate with no natural light. Deep floor plans in excess of 15m window to window are generally unable to provide natural light and natural ventilation, and tend to have wasted space at the centre, which can only be used for storage.

Office workers are not all identical, with identical requirements. The nature of the job and the psychology of the individual give rise to different office "user types". A segmentation analysis of the users of court and MoJ office space has been carried out, which found 5 different "User Types":

It is vital to analyse the users into their user types, both teams and individuals, to be able to provide the correct type of accommodation and office layout. There can be an inadvertent tendency on behalf of the senior executives (decision makers) and project implementation team (project based teams) to assume that everybody else needs what they need.

Research has shown that there is an optimum group size for open plan offices. Office areas, where not cellular, should be defined as bays or rooms with a maximum of 10 people per bay or room, to encourage group working and avoid stifling individuality. The proposed offices at West Bromwich magistrates' court (fig 3.51) offered complex interactive spaces based on the 10-person bay concept. Furniture arrangements and bay size should reflect working patterns, i.e. team working or individual working. Bays should be defined by walls, partitions or furniture. Such bay partitions should be high enough to give visual privacy to the group when seated. The amorphous "battery-farm" image of a call centre should be carefully avoided. Older buildings with load-bearing internal walls need not remain cellular. Larger rooms can be multi occupancy offices. Smaller rooms can be opened up with partition walls remaining to define bays. Previously partitioned large rooms can be re-opened into their original large size as open plan offices.

Fig 3.51 West Bromwich

The most effective workspaces give better performance per person but are not the theoretically most efficient in terms of furniture packing. The effectiveness of an office has to take account of churn cost, health care, retention of key knowledge workers, human capital, job satisfaction, effective ways of working and absenteeism. Very small floor plates have been found to give a high user satisfaction. Too many people in a space has a negative impact on user satisfaction and the effectiveness of a workspace.

Increased creativity is generally considered to be the key benefit target by workplace designers. However, this is not a key concern for courts and MoJ offices, except for a few specialist HQ teams.

Desk shapes have changed over recent years, largely due to changes in technology.

Since the 1960s, desk size and layout has been defined by the needs of the user rather than the seniority of the user. In today's offices space, should be allocated by function, not by hierarchy or equality.

Until the late 1990s desks were large and rectangular usually with a return. The main desk was used for reading and writing documents and for speaking to individuals, who sat on the other side of the desk. The return was used historically for a typewriter, but more recently for a keyboard and monitor. The desk had to be large enough for in and out trays. The L shape enabled the user to swivel from one function to another (typing to reading to discussing to phoning) at a moments' notice. This functionality is still required. With the reduction in size of computers, and particularly of monitors, the return on the desk is now of less necessity, especially if the desk is of adequate length. With the total change to electronic communications, postal in and out trays have become completely redundant in less than a decade, though there is still a requirement for papers on the desk for most people.

Desks that abut each other face to face or at right angles are best where the principal personal interaction is with other people in the team. Desks facing outward to permit someone to informally sit opposite are best where verbal interaction is largely with people specifically coming to speak to the individual.

Bench desking, where rectangular desks are in long straight runs, can be very useful for team working and hot desking. The amount of space occupied by individuals can easily vary day-to-day depending on the particular occupancy and document layout requirements. This has now become the norm.

L shaped desks are still very beneficial where users need to speak with people face to face on a frequent basis, and where a large clutter free desk space is required, free of keyboards, phones, laptops, monitors etc. This would be for functional reasons, e.g. reviewing papers, comparing files, studying drawings or holding meetings. A revival of L shaped desks is envisaged.

Over and above the desking additional furniture is required to make the office a functional and habitable space. Storage is required for filing and should be easily accessible whilst not being located in prime areas. Whilst digital filing is now the norm there is still a requirement for storage of hard copies at point of use within meetings and in court. Where possible, storage should be used to define circulation space and to protect staff from main walkways. Full height storage, whilst efficient is not suitable for use between desks and should be kept to areas not suitable for staff accommodation or against full height partitions. Lower storage (1100mm high) should be used in the main office spaces and where possible should run at 90° to the windows. Staff should also be provided with areas for personal storage. As more desks are shared, the quantity of personal storage per workstation increases. Personal storage relates to the number of staff, not the number of workstations. This can take the form of mobile pedestals underneath desks (becoming less common) or lockers in communal banks.

Screens between desks can be specified as pin boards. A balance needs to be drawn between the need for flexible desking for transient staff (who have little need for pin space), and staff permanently at their desk who can benefit in terms of working efficiency by having pin-up space for each desk, suitable for contact lists, calendar, notes, photos, awards, user name label, etc. However, for information to all staff a centrally located information board (of either pin-able or magnetic material) is useful. The further advantage of pin boards is their acoustic property, absorbing the noise of large open plan offices and improving acoustics, particularly reverberation time.

Additional furniture, including soft seating and small mobile meeting tables located near to areas of desking enable staff to break away from their screens and provide easily accessible space for small meetings. Planting should be considered as an integral part of the office environment and can help control excessively dry humidity levels. However, plants should only be in spaces which are too small for any pieces of furniture.

Physical storage requirements consist of personal storage plus storage dependent on the "user type" and specific job function. Personal storage needs to be lockable and of adequate size to accommodate personal stationery (pencils, pens, rulers, calculator, phone chargers, desk diary, A3 papers, etc.), personal items (handbag, biscuits, spectacles, personal papers, personal medication, etc.) and immediate day files being worked on by the user of the desk plus a laptop computer. Official storage requirements per desk are totally dependant on the nature of the user type and job. Storage will typically be required for A4 paper files, A3 and A4 bound documents, books, and boxes of bound papers or files (e.g. tender submissions or case papers). Such filing should be located within easy reach of the desk, such that the user can reach the papers whilst on the phone. Some user types are best served by group storage/filing, whilst for others working more individually the filing is best on a personal basis. Electronic filing tends to reduce the quantity of long term filing and project based files, but does not eliminate the need for storage of paper documents. Inadequate filing and storage is probably one of the greatest causes of inefficient working.

Since filing requirements relate to the task, not to the number of workstations, space left over by the floor geometry and not large enough for a workstation, should be used for additional storage of the type required by the users. Users requiring the additional storage should be located in the areas where the storage is most efficiently located. Utilising this design logic, additional storage does not reduce the number of workstations possible within the floor plate, it makes more efficient use of the floor plate.

The offices at Westminster magistrates' court manage to utilise the awkward narrow curved space fronting the main road, but thereby benefit from excellent views across the skyline of London. The proposed offices at Wolverhampton magistrates' court offered a dynamic large volume that was the hub of the building and enabled social and functional groupings. (fig 3.52)

Fig 3.52 Wolverhampton

3.3 Detail

3.3.1 Architectural scale

Scale is whether something appears to be large and oppressive or small and intimate, but it is relative, not absolute. The same object, e.g. a 10m high blank wall, can appear large scale or small scale depending on the detailed design. Designers should be conscious of which they want to achieve and not leave it to accident. The wrong scale can be inappropriate, look foolish or oppressive and attract vehement dislike by neighbours.

Perception of scale is dependent on two things: the size of a person relative to the object being viewed, and the effect of light. To quote Protagoras (via Plato and the Prince of Wales) "man is the measure of all things".

On a building, far away a viewer will not see much surface detail, on a surface seen close up a viewer will see a great deal of detail – the texture and pattern of the material, the joints and junctions, the shadows cast by the modelling, the colours of the materials that make up the fabric. If the eye sees little detail the brain assumes the object is far away, from which it judges its size. Therefore, if a building or element of a building has little surface detail it will appear to be larger than it actually is.

This can be deliberate to make the scale large and imposing, as at the courts in Aix en Provence (fig 3.53) or it can be ill considered and make a façade oppressive and prone to graffiti. Some of the brutalist buildings of the 1970s and 1980s made this mistake, such as the former Bristol Magistrates' court and the former Manchester magistrates' court.

Architectural elements can be deliberately made actually larger or smaller than normal, so that when seen next to a person the scale is deliberately distorted. The external staircase at Mold is oversized to make the building more imposing, as are the columns on the Caernarfon Shire hall (fig 3.54), so that the small building on a narrow street can compete with the adjacent castle.

The over-scaled floor to floor heights and lack of detail on the facades of the Nuneaton Justice centre (fig 3.55) can fool people on a drawing, but the reality makes the huge building oppressive in the context of a small market town.

Simple blank glass facades on a street of human scaled 19th century houses would appear out of scale and uncouth. Expressing the structure and even better selecting a structural material of fine detail and character (such as oak) would help match the scale, as at the courts extension in Dijon, France. (fig 3.56)

Fig 3.53 Aix en Provence courthouse

Fig 3.54 Caernarfon

Fig 3.55 Nuneaton

Fig 3.56 Dijon

Where the context is of small buildings, and the court therefore appears large, it is best to break down the mass of the building into various elements of a similar scale to the neighbours, as at Aberystwyth quay side courts (fig 3.57) or Truro Crown Court (fig 3.58).

Fig 3.57 Aberystwyth combined court

Fig 3.58 Truro

Where the context is of large office buildings and massive victorian warehouses, as at Southwark Crown Court (fig 3.59), keeping the small building simple and cubic with minimal detail allows it to compete in scale.

Fig 3.59 Southwark Crown Court

As a useful rule of thumb, to ensure a building appears to be of the correct scale, any piece of the façade the size of a human head should have some detail. This could be the texture and joints of brickwork, the grain of wood or stone, the junctions of framing, the texture of concrete or render, the fixings of cladding, the pattern of tiles and slates, the leaves or shadows of planting, the craftsmanship of artworks, the patina of metals or the view through glass.

Fig 3.60 Peterborough

The magistrates' courts at Peterborough (fig 3.60) have large and potentially brutal modelling, but are brought back to a human scale by the use of brick with careful detailing, set off by the delicate pattern of trees.

3.3.2 EXTERNAL DETAIL

Long life and low maintenance are the key factors for external materials and details. Materials and their details also need to be robust since public buildings such as courts tend to be a target for vandalism, however they must not appear to be robust, since they will then be seen as a challenge to vandals and get even worse attack.

Most details need to derive from functionality. Windows need to be shaded so need deep reveals (as at Newport), overhangs or shade louvres (as at Hendon (fig 3.61).

Main entrance doors need to be boldly emphasised with the architecture leading the eye to the front door, so that visitors can find their way in. Roofs need to be accessible for maintenance, so parapets are useful at the edge of pitched roofs on tall buildings. Ledges need to be avoided to deter roosting birds. Windows need to open for ventilation and cleaning. Pitched roofs are useful to hide rooftop plant. External plant on roofs is a maintenance risk and an eyesore, so needs to be internal or hidden by roof detailing (as at Liverpool QE2 courts) (fig 3.62).

Fig 3.61 Hendon

Fig 3.62 Liverpool

Graffiti artists need to be kept away from buildings, so railings are often placed about a metre away from facades.

Sometimes special details are required for special situations. The integrated high level air intake louvres on the Manchester CJC (fig 3.63) are a good example, where the prevailing wind had to be utilised for natural ventilation over 100m above ground level.

Fig 3.63 Manchester CJC *Fig 3.64 Truro*

Sometimes the details need to be developed as part of a particular architectural requirement determined by a challenging site. The conical roofscape at Truro (fig 3.64), which was built on the site of the former castle at the highest point in the town, is a notable example.

Local materials are also often rightly insisted upon by local authorities, such as the slate at Caernarfon and the hard shiny coal-measure brick at Newport (fig 3.65).

Fig 3.65 Newport brick detail

3.3.3 Interior design

The interior design of most buildings is to do with the materials and furnishings, these however are fairly standard in court buildings. The size and shape of the court rooms and offices are also fairly standard. This means that the form and volume of the spaces, the sequence of spaces and the quality of natural light are the key determinants of interior design in law courts. These in turn tend to be determined or instigated by the tight and awkward sites that courts tend to inhabit, which dictate the plans, and thus the nature of the key spaces.

The courtrooms and the entrance/courthall are the key spaces for interior design. The position of the natural light is often the dominant design factor.

In a court room the light may come from clerestorey windows, a glazed rooflight, from roof slots allowing the light to stream down the walls, from glazed walls, from punched windows, or from concealed slots of in baffled walls. The modelling of the ceiling, and the use of acoustic panels on the walls, use and diffuse the light.

Fig 3.66 Southampton

Southampton (fig 3.66), Leamington, Peterborough, Derby, Lincoln and the Supreme Court show the range of courtroom interior design, thought they are all based on the same plan.

In the court hall, which is often an atrium incorporating the entrance and all waiting areas, this is often the most dramatic space in a court building. There are open airy atria such as Manchester CJC where the whole city is laid out before you (fig 3.67), or spacious but intimate barn-like spaces, such as Lincoln magistrates' court where users are given tantalising glimpses of the old city outside. Huntingdon gives a huge framed picture of a tree outside, whilst Truro (fig 3.68) creates a white sculptural model of the hilltop which you must climb to reach the courts.

Fig 3.67 Manchester

Office areas, including judges' retiring suites are simple rooms with modern corporate office furniture, and no aspirations to interior design.

Court buildings have a myriad of small rooms, and the large rooms such as courtrooms have a myriad of doors. Corridors need to be closed off for separate circulation. This means that courthalls and all circulation areas have a plethora of doors. For security reasons, many of these doors are not labelled, except to exclude the public. A key interior design factor is therefore making logical sense of all the doors. This is done by having a hierarchy of doors in the public areas. A courtroom public entrance should like more important than an office entrance, which in turn should look more important than a cupboard or duct door. The hierarchy is achieved by door finishes, door surrounds, integrated signage, door size, glazing, door furniture and locational prominence. Manchester CJC and Hendon achieve this well (fig 3.69).

Fig 3.68 Truro interior

Fig 3.69 Hendon

3.3.4 Interior materials

The design and materials used in the construction of a courthouse should be of good quality, long lasting and free of gimmicks. Ostentation must be avoided. A courthouse is a civic building but its function is strictly utilitarian. There is no place for extravagance or the overt opulence which is sometimes seen as the expression of a successful commercial undertaking.

Court buildings contain a number of broadly defined areas within which the functions carried out call for standards of finish and characteristics which are consistent with that function.

Traditionally types of room were grouped with regard to the robustness and dignity required of the finishes:

Courtrooms: High quality and of a nature to reflect the dignity of the Judicial process.

Jury Assembly: Good quality and appearance, analogous to a Hotel Lounge/Coffee Shop.

Assembly areas, public, legal profession, concourses, dining rooms: Hard wearing but good appearance.

Judicial/Magistrates' area, general offices and staff amenities: Good functional standard as for commercial offices.

Custody: Specialised finishes

Plantrooms, bulk storerooms etc: Basic sound finish.

There has been a trend towards the most simple and basic finishes. Walls are almost without exception white painted plaster, since this can be redecorated easily if marked. Ceilings are either white painted plaster or exposed concrete to exploit their thermal capacity, suspended ceilings are very rarely used. Doors and furniture are real wood veneers since these can be re-finished if marked and are cheaper than plastic imitation finishes. Floors are carpet tile for ease of replacement and cleaning, except in courthalls and entrance areas, where they are terrazzo, stone or ceramic tiles to resist wear and wet footprints. Glass and stainless steel tends to be used for balustrades and screens, such as secure docks.

Custody areas have specialised finishes to avoid the extremely onerous attempts at vandalism, escape and self harm. However, they do not need to be as secure against long term attack as prisons, nor as proof against graffiti and bodily fluids as police cells.

Courtroom materials should be appropriate for the dignified character of courtrooms while at the same time being restful on the eye and most importantly providing appropriate acoustic conditions. Walls should, as far as possible, be of low maintenance materials with suitable acoustic qualities. Smooth, shiny surfaces and rough-textured surfaces should be avoided (the latter particularly in the dock). Suggested finishes include light wood panelling and furniture, contrasting seating fabrics (eg scarlet, royal blue or dark green) and toning carpet. The budget is unlikely to be adequate to allow timber panelling throughout but should enable selected parts to be finished in timber for acoustics and to delineate the hierarchy of the courtroom. Richly-figured veneer panelling and very pale wood finishes should be avoided. Care should also be taken to avoid the problems of eyestrain caused by vertical lines in acoustic strip panelling, or other striped or heavily-patterned finishes.

Gee St Courthouse in Clerkenwell London (fig 3.70) shows good examples of the new aesthetic of simple furniture in a robust exposed concrete historic warehouse reused as a court building, with insertion of acoustic panels and exploitation of character, texture and geometry.

Fig 3.70 Gee Street

3.3.5 Internal detailing

The detailing within court buildings should be simple, elegant and robust. Public areas of the court building will get heavy usage by customers who are less than careful and often wish to deliberately damage the building in which they are prosecuted.

It is better to have finishes and details that are easy to repair, than details that try to look un-damageable. Details that look as though they are designed to be un-damageable are just seen as a challenge to dedicated vandals. For instance, banks of heavy chairs linked together as at Nuneaton magistrates court (fig 3.71) look elegant but can never be thrown around.

Fig 3.71 Nuneaton

The judicial and other private areas will have constant use over many years (the average life of a court building is 100 years) so only robust details for items such as door handles and stair balustrades will last the test of time, as 19th century details have done. Solid timber architraves and skirtings will easily last 100 years, whereas MDF mouldings will be destroyed as soon as they get wet or need adjusting.

The extent of suspended floors to permit flexible layouts for electrical power/IT requirements should be examined on a scheme-by-scheme basis, as they add substantially to project costs. Similarly, proposals for electrical power/IT flood wiring or trunking layouts should be developed individually for each scheme. Power outlets are required on both sides of the clerk's bench for equipment used by the clerk/shorthand writer. Power points will also be needed in or near the area occupied by the judge, jury, witnesses, counsel and defendant(s) since IT equipment is ubiquitous.

Detailing for easy maintenance is important for reduced running costs. For instance, light fittings over stairs tend to need scaffold access to change the luminaire. They should be located where the ceiling is normal height, or if this is unavoidable they should be fitted with long life luminaires such as LED which have a 15-year life.

Detailing for disability is important. This is to do with such items as visible or tactile stair nosings and contrast colours for signage. This should not be considered an afterthought with black and yellow sticky tape everywhere. Careful selection of materials and details will ensure suitability for people with disabilities or injuries (who are more common than normal in courts and particularly tribunals) whilst still producing an elegant building for the majority of users.

3.3.6 Colour

There is now very little colour used in court buildings. The traditional red of the upholstery of the seats in a Crown court tends to remain, but is the only major colour still used. The upholstery of other courts tends to be black, but can be any dark colour. Virtually all painted finishes are white. Pale wood veneers and stainless steel tend to be the only other colours in court buildings. Coloured feature walls can be helpfully used to define large spaces, e.g. in offices, or to differentiate between different floors or zones in large buildings.

The one exception to the general white and wood appearance of court building interiors is the Royal Coat of Arms. This is required to be displayed above and behind the Judge or magistrate in every courtroom, and also externally at the building entrance, normally on the façade above the main entrance. It is necessary to ensure that its function of indicating the representation of the Sovereign is heraldically correct within the context of the material employed. Some artistic licence is permissible in adjusting the proportions of the design to suit a particular situation, or of the finer details to suit a particular material (fig. 3.72).

Fig 3.72 Leamington 1950s enamel coat of arms

The coat of arms need not be coloured, but where the arms are to be coloured, the colouring of the Royal Arms should conform to the following schedule, which is in non-heraldic language for simplicity:

Red, Vermilion
Velvet of all crowns; extreme right and left gems in bands of crowns and of coronet on neck of unicorn; tongue and claws of lion surrounding crown; spaces in visor of helmet; background of the two lion quarters of shield; surrounds and fleur de lys of Scottish quarter of shield; tongue and claws of supporting lion; tongue of unicorn; body and tail of Scottish lion; outer ring of petals of roses (or all petals if only one ring).

Blue, Royal or Ultramarine
Background of garter; middle gems in bands of all crowns and of coronet on neck of unicorn; tongues and claws of all lions on shield; reverse of scroll.

Blue, Cerulean or Cobalt
Background of harp quarter of shield; face of scroll.

Green, Emerald
Gems on either side of centre in bands of crowns and of coronet on beck of unicorn; ground on which supporting lion and unicorn stand.

Green, Mid-Brunswick
Stalks, leaves and sepals of roses and thistles; stalks and leaves of shamrock.

Purple, Royal
Petals of thistles.

Gold or Yellow
Supporting and surmounting lions; helmet; lettering, buckle and eyelets of garter; clasp and ornament on tip of belt below garter; background of Scottish lion quarter of shield; scroll and garet edgings and motto lettering; horn, hoofs, mane, collar, chain, tufts on tail, chest and flanks of unicorn; face of mantling to helmet; body of harp; centre of roses.

Silver or White
Body of unicorn, including stem of tail; reverse of mantling to helmet (marked as ermine in black); wreaths at bases of crowns (marked as ermine); strings of harp; inner ring of petals of roses.

3.3.7 Environmental quality

Environmental conditions for lighting and ventilation within the court building and in the courtrooms in particular are of great importance and care must be taken to ensure that the criteria specified in the MoJ data sheets are achieved. Natural lighting (i.e. daylight) and natural ventilation (i.e. opening windows usually) are to be provided. Air-conditioning is to be provided only if it is unavoidable. Mixed solutions, where chilling and fresh air equipment is provided, are acceptable and normal, but it only needs to be used at critical times of day and extremes of weather throughout the year. Controls need to be used to ensure this is the case.

Natural ventilation is brought about by the 'stack effect' which may be assisted by the wind. The stack effect is the name given to the movement of air driven by a temperature difference between inside and outside air. Natural ventilation is limited to the supply of sufficient fresh air to give comfortable conditions for the occupants. It will not provide cooling in summer, unless there is a source of cool air, such as from underground ducts or a cool basement. In winter conditions, supplied air will require heating.

To rely on a natural process to achieve ventilation of a courtroom means that it will not be possible to control temperature, humidity and noise precisely. A mechanically ventilated or air conditioned courtroom is sealed against changes in outside conditions and provides full control over these parameters. With natural ventilation, it is predicted that during an average summer (June, July, August) with average occupancy, there is a risk that overheating may occur for three hours on six days per month. (Overheating in excess of 26°C.) The environmental services and management of the building should be designed to handle this. In order to create the stack effect, it is necessary to provide low level inlets and high level outlets. Windows will be the normal means of providing outlets. Opening a window to give ventilation may raise internal noise levels. It is not possible to generalise on the extent to which the internal noise level within the courtroom will be raised as this will depend on the particular noise conditions affecting the site. This will be established by a noise survey. In principal, the building should be designed to provide the necessary opening windows in quiet site areas, sheltered acoustically by the building mass.

Natural ventilation is driven by the temperature difference between the inside and outside, but is also a function of the distance between inlets and outlets, known as the 'stack height'. A courtroom that cannot accommodate a stack height of 5m should not rely on achieving ventilation by the stack effect. A courtroom height of 6m should therefore be regarded as a minimum. Courtrooms which are higher than 6m will benefit from a greater air flow rate. However, design teams will need to balance this benefit with the cost of providing the additional building height and its appropriateness to the overall design. The inlets and outlets need not be within the room height. Inlets below floor level and outlets in chimneys, ventilation shafts or light slots above the ceiling can achieve the stack effect height required, e.g. Lincoln and Bournemouth.

There are five types of lighting, but unfortunately engineers tend to only think of ambient lighting to give a certain illumination level. Interior designers consider all types of lighting to best enhance the space for its function. Older buildings can achieve the greatest benefit from well-considered lighting. The types of lighting are:

- Ambient lighting
- Accent lighting
- Task lighting
- Decorative lighting
- Kinetic lighting

Ambient lighting is the general illumination level typically provided by fluorescent or LED ceiling lights in offices or tungsten light bulbs in homes, or street lights externally.

Accent lighting is a spot light or downlight or wall washer to draw attention to a part of the room or a feature, to give liveliness to an interior, or to visually alter the volume of a space or position of a wall. It enhances the perception of form. It is used in reception areas, restaurants, living rooms and public buildings, and is the key approach for external floodlighting of buildings.

Task lighting gives specific light to a specific task, such as down lights over a cooking area or a desk lamp, or spot lights to show off a picture or externally a sign.

Decorative lighting gives off little illumination but looks pretty. Crystal or brass chandeliers, table lamps with ornamental shades, lava lamps or converted gas wall lights or historic street lights would fall into this category. They are popular in the domestic market and in pubs and restaurants, but are probably limited to historic light fixtures in court buildings.

Kinetic lighting is moving light, as given off by an open fire or the reflected sunlight off water or dappled sunlight seen through trees, or the reflection of a building in a river. It is the most welcoming and relaxing of light.

Not all types of lighting are required in all buildings or rooms. Living rooms, restaurants, art galleries, museums and public spaces would require all of them, but utilitarian spaces like plantrooms and factories would only need ambient light. The more detailed the interior design the more good lighting will enhance it. Older court buildings, and particular their courtrooms and public spaces would benefit greatly from having at least 4 of the 5 types of lighting. Important historic or modern buildings benefit from all types of lighting externally.

3.3.8 Appearance of security features

It is inappropriate for security reasons to discuss what security is required in a court building. It is a cardinal principle of good security that protection must be proportionate to the risk. Overprotection, with its implied waste of resources, can be as bad as under-protection. A realistic assessment of the risk should help to avoid this.

In principle, a building that tries to look as if it is important and secure is more likely to be targeted. Some court buildings are important due to their function, others are important due to their location. There can be a conflict between wanting to make a court building appear friendly and welcoming (to encourage witnesses etc.) and the necessary security precautions of any modern public building.

The ideal is for the building to be inherently secure and to play down the appearance of any security provision. For example, a glass façade can be friendly and welcoming and symbolise open justice, but it would be easy to ram raid a vehicle through it. If the structural floor slab is a few 100 mm above the pavement line no vehicle could penetrate the glass façade. Similarly, if there was a risk of vehicles accidentally hitting a glass front on a busy road the ornamental potted plants and sofas just inside the glass front could actually be a vehicle barrier to protect people inside.

Exposed columns on the outside of a building, e.g. as a colonnade, can appear to be a simple target for deliberate or accidental damage. The uncouth solution is to make them big and chunky enough to stop any damage. The more elegant solution usually adopted by engineers is to incorporate structural redundancy so that removing a column will not threaten the structural integrity of the building.

The main entrance can be considered to be a high-risk area. A flight of steps up to the main entrance is a traditional architectural detail for a public building, but has gone out of fashion for disability reasons. It has now been found that this detail is excellent for preventing ram raiding, drive by shootings, motorbike mugging, suicide bombings, etc. where crowds of people gather to enter public buildings. The detail is being revived, e.g. Leamington and Chester magistrates' courts (fig 3.73).

At one time bollards and planters were springing up around public buildings. Now such vehicle barriers are being replaced with changes of level, moats and integrated benches within the landscape. These are equally as effective but less visually obtrusive and more friendly to the public, e.g. Newport and the Supreme Court (fig 3.74).

Fig 3.73 Chester magistrates' court

Fig 3.74 Supreme Court

Ultimately the natural defences of cliffs and rivers to prevent people approaching may well make a comeback, as may the hairpin approach paths and blank robust lower walls of castles, which occurred on the site for Sunderland. (fig 3.75)

Fig 3.75 Sunderland site for proposed new court

4. Portfolio of examples 2000 - 2015

4.1 New court buildings

4.1.1 Cambridge County Court

Cambridge County Court is on an infill site where the ring road meets the historic centre at Parker's Piece – one of the green lungs of Cambridge, which is surrounded not by academia but by public buildings and shops. The County Court sits between a church and the fire station, with the police station, swimming pool, hotel, bus station and shopping centre for company around the large grassy field of Parker's Piece.

The function of a county Court is to handle family and business disputes. The justice is low key, nobody is guilty of anything,, there is no right and wrong party, just settlement of private disputes. The building is therefore low key – quiet but elegant. It looks like an office block. It is a simple modernist frame infilled with glass and enlivened with a flurry of louvred sun shades, echoing the dappled shade of the trees it overlooks in this leafy corner of Cambridge.

Architect's CGI image

Looking towards Parker's Piece

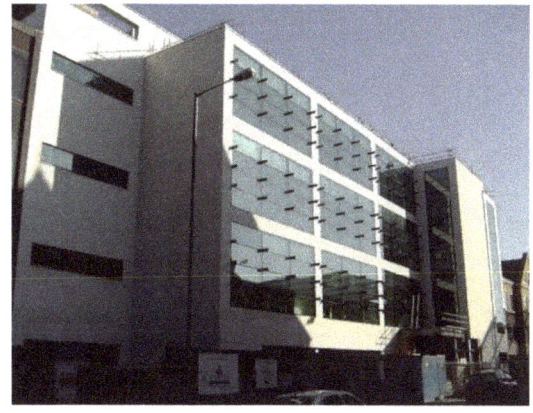

Main frontage nearing completion

4.1.2 Manchester magistrates' court

Manchester magistrates' court was built by a developer as part of the enabling development for a new business quarter in Manchester. It is unusual in that it had to work as a court building, with a properly accessible street frontage, whilst everything else around it was excavated away and rebuilt.

The court building is located above shops, and is approached as the termination to a new street flanked by the restored historic University library and a shiny new Norman Foster office building. The building is planned as two linear wings (one side court rooms and the other side offices) separated by a tall long atrium. This is expressed on the outside as two solid masonry blocks separated by a glass wall, and dominated by an axial escalator taking users up 6m from the street to the raised ground floor. It is in effect a dynamic extension of the newly created street.

The rear elevation, onto a public square and facing the 1950s Crown court, is an echo of the front elevation. However, here the atrium does not reach the ground, due to falls in the ground level and the shop frontages. Instead, the end of the atrium is a glass winter garden with palm trees, hanging dramatically halfway up the façade. Sadly this startling elevation may get hidden by further development, and only be seen from the top of the Manchester Civil Justice Centre looming a block away.

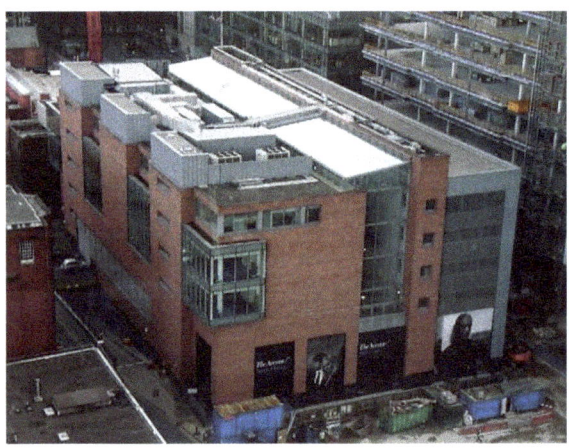

Manchester magistrates' court seen from judges' dining room of Manchester Civil Justice Centre. Note courts to left of atrium and offices to right.

Perspective

Interior of atrium   *Entrance elevation*

4.1.3 Huntingdon

Huntingdon magistrates' court forms part of a larger civic complex built as a PDS (private developer scheme) on backland in the heart of the ancient market town behind the 18th century townhouses that many years ago became the town hall and civic offices. The complex consists of the courts, new council offices, a public library and the bus station. The complex uses new buildings to weave together the historic buildings, the mature trees from the remains of the 18th century gardens, the space left over from the construction of the inner ring road, and the wasteland that for years had been car parking and an accumulation of civic centre accretions.

The old court was over the market hall. A fine Georgian building, but where the open arcaded market had been gradually in-filled to provide the back office accommodation, and the courtrooms themselves had been chopped up for retiring and consultation rooms. Court users will change from being stressed by being squashed into tiny dark rooms amongst the market traders to being calmed down by sitting in a tranquil sun dappled courthall nestling amongst the trees, yet only a minute away from the market square.

General view from inner ring road

Rear elevation

Interior of courtroom *View from atrium out to the trees*

Entrance elevation

Former courthouse, open arcade infilled

4.1.4 WORLE

Worle magistrates' court is unusual in that although it replaces a tired court building in the centre of the seaside resort of Weston Super Mare, it is actually located on a greenfield site in a location that only dreams of one day being an urban centre. Worle magistrates' court is located next to the Worle Parkway station in an area zoned for light industry, retail sheds and housing – most of which has yet to be built. The new court therefore has to try to be the first building to give Worle an urban and civic identity.

The main building has a concave form with two wings enclosing a circular civic plaza – the first piece of urban public space in Worle. The hard landscaping, seats and sculpture form a suitable calm and relaxing urban space leading to the courts. The unusual use of local random rubble stonework for the building contrasts with the shimmering curved glazing. The materials are frugal but charming and their unexpected presence gives a strikingly different feel from the tin sheds of the light industrial units and retail sheds which surround it, and which were built to the same budget.

The separation of the office functions into a simple but elegant rectangular brick box next door gives two urbanising buildings for the price of one, whilst keeping costs down. This is a remarkable, friendly and surprising building, urbanising the new town of Worle, and still waiting at the train station for the rest of the town to arrive.

Civic entrance courtyard

Courtroom interior

Administration block to rear

4.1.5 Exeter Crown court

The dramatic white and silver cone of roof of Exeter Crown Court can be glimpsed over the roofs from all over Exeter, signifying its civic importance. Bizarrely, having been located in Exeter's Rougemont castle since 1068 the courts had always been hidden from public view. Nobody even knew the castle was there. The new courts are located on backland at the edge of the historic core of this ancient city, but the site backs onto the ring road too. The frontage opens onto a formal Georgian tree lined avenue, built apparently on the line of the old town walls. It is set back in the sun beyond the trees and in its scale and form it echoes the adjoining Georgian terraces and Regency villas.

Visually it is 2 storey double fronted villa with a rectangular office bay to the left, a central entrance opening into an atrium, and a circular bay to the right crowned by a dramatic conical lantern, capping the circular courtroom. The white stucco makes the building stand out in the gloom of the shady avenue. From the rear the building is dramatically different. The topography falls away to give a four storey building, with its row of silo-like courtroom drums towering over the tiny mews cottages in the valley below, perhaps an echo of its old castle home. The service elevations to the ring road are a plain non-descript modern office building.

The plan is a simple linear arrangement. A long atrium, glazed at both ends, has a row of courtrooms of courtrooms in circular drums to one side, and offices to the other side. It is exactly what the main elevation leads you to expect, and far more welcoming than is old home in a high security Norman castle.

Front elevation;   *glimpse from historic core of Exeter*

Interior of courtroom courts;   *building in context*

Entrance rotunda from ring road ; rear elevation

4.1.6 Bristol Magistrates' court

Bristol magistrates' court is the epitome of the complex mixed use required for inner city sites in the 21st century. The site has to not only accommodate the magistrates' and coroners' courts, but also a bus station, student housing and a small shopping centre. It has to squeeze between the ring road and a medieval abbey, whilst re-establishing the ancient street pattern for the pedestrian route into the retail heart of the city, and coping with steep falls across the site and archaeology beneath the ground.

It is astonishing that anyone could fit it all in, and a great pleasure to realise the challenge has resulted in excellent architecture and a rewarding piece of real city.

It is a linear building, slicing one side off the site, and planned as a series of slivers of space – public, courts, judicial circulation, atrium, offices. The acute angled front façade reveals the slices and terminates in a crisp knife edge arris to sharply mark the entrance. At night it shimmers to even more clearly display the form.

This is no architectural affectation. The multiple functions of the site required three long thin slices of buildings. The noise and pollution of the bus station requires a blank wall with an atrium for light air and security. The tightness of the site forced the building to reach into every available corner of the site. Easy sites make for bland buildings; this is a classic example of an almost impossible set of problems leading to excellent architecture. A challenge brings out the best in an architect.

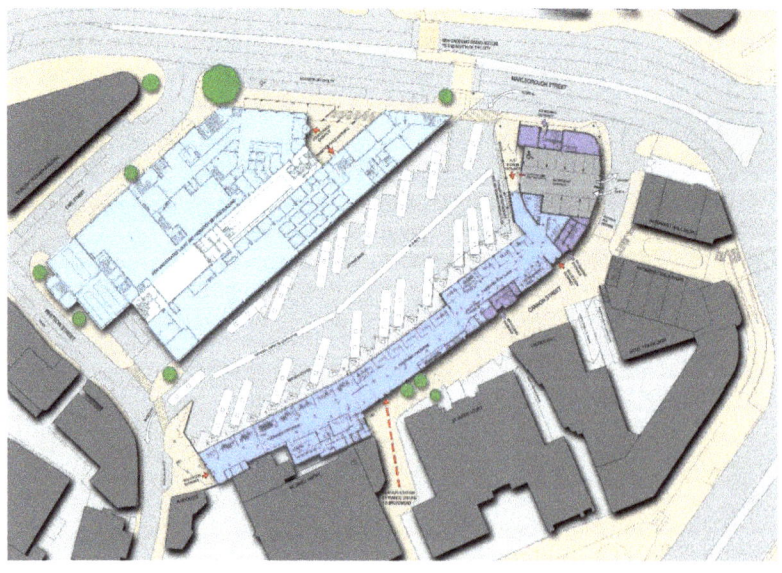

Site plan

 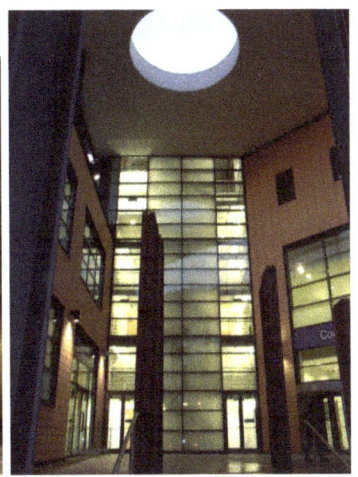

Main entrance *Entrance and atrium*

Approach view at arris

Bus station frontage; *side view*

4.1.7 Cambridge Crown Court

The first impression of Cambridge Crown court is of a hard circular fortress tower – a modernist bastion or block house on the ring road, marking the edge of town. The form derives from its location: the site is almost an island, a bulging peninsular of left-over land formed when the ring road cut through the existing road network. The environment is harsh – a ring road, a traffic junction, the rear delivery bays of a shopping centre, a run down secondary retail terrace. But hidden amongst the dross are some fine Georgian houses that have seen better days, some sturdy Victorian non-conformist chapels and some pleasant mature trees which are probably the remains from the lost large academics' houses from the mid19th century.

The court building has to protect the users against the perceived harsh environment and the actual air and noise pollution of the exposed site. Symbolically it is appropriate to express such a criminal court as a bastion of justice against the crime of the world. Architecturally it gives a pavilion like building reinstating the suburban streetscape of detached houses, public buildings and terraces of shops, all set amongst the trees of suburban Cambridge. The street is slowly becoming urban again, no longer a lost corner of the city.

Internally it is not as hard as the outside; it peels open like a piece of fruit to show off its soft interior. The slots of the "gun emplacements" are then revealed as clerestorey lighting to the courtrooms. The courtrooms pick up some of the curves but are basically as rectangular as their function, with the poché taking up all the minor functions.

The courts in the bleak ring road context. The hard skin peels away for the entrance.

"Hard circular fortress"   Main entrance

4.1.8 LOUGHBOROUGH MAGISTRATES' COURT

The award winning Loughborough magistrates' court is a simple and elegant box, which becomes more sophisticated and elegant the closer you look. The plan is a classic 2 storey linear design, but with clever rooflights to bring daylight into the depth of the building, and a veil of brise soleil to control heat and light whilst visually enhancing the façade. The carefully considered external lighting gives drama at night and highlights the nature of the project as a public building whilst enhancing the public linear park created to link up the various parts of the town centre through this redevelopment area.

The end street façade expresses the cross section of the linear design and gives a building of appropriate scale and proportion for an historic street within this old university town. In contrast, the very long frontage to the new public space (which may one day become an inner ring road) defines a new urban character appropriate to the new urban quarter being created within an old hospital site. The building's dynamism, functionality and urban qualities belie the fact that this is one of the cheapest new court buildings built in the last decade. It is not big budgets that produce design excellence, it is talented and keen designers.

Front elevation to new square

End elevation to street; courtroom interior

Night elevation of entrance

4.1.9 Cambridge magistrates' court

Cambridge magistrates' court used to be in a quiet elegant 1970s landscaped quadrangle building, just like a modern college, but bizarrely located on top of a multi-storey carpark and only accessible from a dustbin yard via a urine soaked and graffiti covered lift. The owners of the adjacent shopping centre wanted to extend by redeveloping the carpark and other retail premises on the High St. They offered to replace the magistrates' court in a more suitable location.

After an extensive search for suitable sites, eventually it was decided to again use the upper floors of the shopping centre, even though this required the construction of a temporary court building at a park-and-ride site at Trumpington on the edge of town.

The new courts are on the upper floors of the shopping centre, with rooflights to the courtrooms and windows looking into the buzz of life in the atrium of the shopping centre below, and also looking over the High St and Parker's Piece.

The novel aspect is the frontage. As part of the shopping centre a fine and rather grand Listed Victorian building had to be retained. It had been built as a high-class dressmakers, with an elegant classical display room for private customers on the first floor, but had long been incorporated into a department store. This building has been restored and forms the public face to the courts. The narrow 5 storey sliver of a building gives a suitably imposing frontage for a public building, whilst giving modern facilities behind, largely on a single level for convenience. The public enter off the street in a building very different from its retail neighbours. They are sped up to roof level for the airy courts, with the historic street frontage rooms used for consultation and meetings. For the public it is architecturally a distinctive public building of character integrated into the heart of the city. Practically, it has all the modern facilities required, integrated with the functionality and well organised servicing of a shopping centre.

Temporary prefab courts

Historic front elevation; street context

Courts elevation within shopping centre

4.1.10 Manchester Civil Justice Centre

Manchester CJC is probably the most well known new law court built this century. It is one of the most prominent buildings in Manchester and had, at last count, won 28 design awards, including being runner-up for the Stirling Prize. It is the largest new court building built in Britain for 150 years. The story behind its purpose is fascinating.

This is not a criminal court, it only handles Civil, Family and Commercial cases. The courts for such cases are (theoretically) self financing through court fees, but at the same time disputes between businesses (especially international businesses) are highly lucrative for the legal industry and the UK economy.

Manchester CJC was built not only to handle local family and business matters more efficiently, but primarily to attract international business to Britain, through having international contracts written under English law. The grandeur of the Royal Courts of Justice was traditionally good for attracting international business, but the move of business into digital technology required a more cutting edge and high profile approach. Manchester CJC was built to achieve this.

An international design competition was launched, allied to a PFI developer, who was required to take on the winning design (thus retaining the best and losing the worst aspects of PFI). The winners were Denton Corker Marshall, an acclaimed Australian practice who had come to Britain after winning the Stonehenge visitor centre competition. They were appalled at the high cost of English commercial architecture, so used Australian approaches to design to achieve an economical but stunning design solution.

At the local level, MCJC has been very successful in using architecture to exploit psychology to resolve case more equitably and quickly. Parties can find the building easily due to its prominence, and since the front door was put on the tip of the site where it touches the main artery of the city at the bridge head. They can find their way around the building easily, due to the simple linear plan and everything opening off and seen from the atrium, into which the front door enters. This reduces the stress for parties. The airy waiting spaces, day lit courtrooms and stunning views over the city give a calming and distracting feel. This de-stressing of the parties in family cases has been particularly noticed by the judges, who recognise that cases in this building are more easily and quickly resolved, with less anger and violence in court. Family cases take 10 -15% less time to resolve due to the architecture.

Environmentally the building is also a tour-de-force. When built it was the largest and tallest naturally ventilated building in Europe. It exploits the prevailing wind which is quite fierce on such a tall slab block on an exposed site next to the river. The building is ventilated by the multitude of slots in the solid façade abutting the atrium which use the wind to feed fresh air across every floor and through every courtroom. The atrium acts as a buffer to the main part of the building to minimise heating costs, and its 1m wide gap between the inner and outer panes of the double glazing act as a perfect stack effect chimney to avoid the need for chillers for cooling. The individually fine tuned louvre screens on the opposite façade shelter each room from overheating due to morning sun in the summer, yet encourage ambient solar gain in winter.

The atrium is the space which astounds. It is all frameless glass and steel 60m high and 63m long – the largest glass wall in Europe. People lean their heads back so far to see the top that they almost fall over backwards. If you have the nerve you can walk on the open mesh walkways within the double glazing (known jovially as the "walk of death") with no visual barrier above or below or to either side of you. The finesse of the detailing makes you feel you are literally walking in the air, with Manchester laid out before you somewhere below the clouds.

Manchester CJC from the Irwell Bridge at night showing main entrance

Cantilevered courtrooms

Atrium, wind powered air intakes and cantilevered courtrooms from NW

Inside the atrium

Inside the air intakes

Courtroom

Judges' lounge

Town Hall view from waiting area, note diagonal bracing that supports cantilevered courtrooms

South elevation; East elevation – detail of intricate adjustable perforated screen to give summer shading and winter ambient solar gain

4.1.11 Salisbury

Salisbury is a fine and important historic market town, the sort of place that has been the seat of local justice for 1000 years. As with many such locations, justice was carried out in a variety of buildings, both historic and mundane. The historic Shire Hall, as is often the case, was built for a multitude of functions – a meeting place for the community and the town council, a place for celebrations such as wedding banquets, and the formal location for justice when the judge visited every quarter. The mundane was a group of unsuitable 1950s former military offices, converted into courts.

The new building is built just outside the city walls. It is in an area of fine Georgian merchant houses backing onto the countryside, which had been overwhelmed by hospital buildings in the last half century. As the hospital moves out to modern more hygienic facilities the quality of the environment of this Georgian suburb can once again be appreciated, and the holes in the urban fabric can be patched by new buildings such as these courts.

The site is on one of the historic tree lined roads entering the town from the countryside. It has a series of large detached Georgian, Regency and Victorian villas set back from the road. The new building echoes this form: a simple brick and render building on a slight podium with the modest proportions of its Georgian precedents, but in a modern idiom. As a building it reinstates the townscape damaged by a long lost predecessor, as a law court it reinstates the quality of justice that had been inhibited by using unsuitable older buildings.

Design perspective

As built

Courts in urban context; side elevation with courts to L and offices to R

Window detail

4.1.12 CAERNARFON CRIMINAL COURTS

The new Crown and Magistrates' court at Caernarfon replaces a Georgian Shire Hall next to the castle, which had been built as a theatre (with fly tower and proscenium arch) but never used as such. A clever new entrance and re-organisation of the circulation had extended its life by 20 years, but the inability of modern custody vans to get through the medieval gates to the fortified town meant a new court building was needed.

The new court sits on a hill above the town next to the Roman fort, yet only a few minutes walk up from the market place and castle. It has two wings, one containing the offices and one for the courtrooms. This gave notable cost savings, as did re-using the stone from the old school on the site for landscape retaining walls. This is a frugal but elegant building.

No specific civic grandeur is required here. Just the physical size of the building makes it stand out from the predominantly 2 storey market town. Internally the use of a dramatic sweeping stair set within a triple height space dominated by a wall of slate makes users well aware that this is the one building in the town that is as important as the castle.

One gets the impression that the Welsh see historic buildings as the past, and just for tourists. They want new buildings for use by the Welsh populace to be modern. The new restaurants serving the best of Welsh food and the arts centre showing the best of Welsh music and drama show this tendency. The courts certainly have the drama of the best modern architecture. The (Welsh trained) American architects have brought a touch of international sensibility and sophistication to this remote harbour town, just as when the Romans built their fort and the Normans built their castle here. Perhaps internationally Caernarfon is not considered to be such a remote backwater as the English might think.

General view – projecting courtrooms behind glazed foyer, office wing behind to left

Court room; grand stair in triple height entrance hall

Entrance in context; approach up the hill from the town

4.1.13 Leamington Spa Justice Centre

Functionally, this one of the most unusual and innovative court buildings of recent years. It not only has Crown, County and Magistrates' courts, but also police, probation, youth offending team, Crown Prosecution Service and in fact all the agencies of the entire justice system integrated under one roof. The idea of a seamless justice system was the idea of the Chief Constable of the Warwickshire Constabulary, who led the project and was strongly supported by the Lord Chancellor's Dept (later MoJ). There are actually two Warwickshire Justice Centres, one in Nuneaton and the main one in Leamington Spa.

The complexity of the project meant that the project was neither quick nor cheap, but the result at Leamington is excellent, both for justice and as a piece of architecture.

Finding a suitable site was difficult. Over 20 sites were considered, in and around Warwick and Leamington. The magistrates had been in Leamington and Stratford upon Avon, the Crown court had been in the historic Grade 1 Listed buildings in Warwick. The police were in Warwick, Leamington and Kenilworth. The customers for the magistrates' courts tended to come from the estates south of Leamington. The sites considered included land fronted by a medieval leper hospital, a rare Georgian gas holder, an industrial estate next to a foundry, railway sidings, and the Regency terraces of the Spa. Eventually it was decided that the building was best located in the town centre of Leamington.

The site is in the heart of the Regency conservation area, overlooking the Jephson Botanical Gardens and the town hall. It was occupied by the former police station, Ministry of Agriculture offices, and magistrates' courts complex from the 1960s, which had been likened to a concrete bungalow. The new building reinstates the scale, form, proportions and materials of the Regency buildings by Nash that had been destroyed in a bombing raid during the war. It is a key site where the grand stucco terraces of the Regency planned town open out onto the sylvan landscape of the spa gardens parkland, dotted with its elegant villas, follies and pavilions.

At the entrance the steps and ramp form a podium, which leads into the atrium entrance hall. The huge coat of arms symbolically celebrates that this is a public building as important as the Spa Baths which it faces across the park. Internally the atrium gives views across the park from all the public waiting spaces.

The internal planning is what is unusual about this building. The logical U shaped arrangement of courts surrounding the public space, with the judicial space beyond, is not unusual. However the layout of some of the courtrooms is novel. The historic Crown Courts at Warwick were very intimate, octagonal and top lit. The parties sat round a central table with the public in a gallery above the courtroom. This had worked well for 200 years and the judge quite rightly saw no reason to abandon the concept. With the will to achieve this unusual design it was found to be perfectly possible to achieve the layout and ambience whilst complying with the current design standards.

The other unusual design feature is the office floor. The existing former police station and the main office floor were designed to act as one huge open plan ring of office floor, with two light wells and views all around. The agencies all sit together, sequenced so that they are in the order in which they handle the case: police then CPS then magistrates then Crown court then social services then custody then probation then back round again. The youth and adult services run in parallel, so that as defendants move from youth through to adulthood their cases and records are not dissipated and lost. The process is much more efficient and leads to better justice.

Courts in context of Regency Leamington Spa

Main elevation facing Jephson Gardens

Side elevation including van dock

Double height Crown court showing public gallery and central table

Court room furniture enquiries desk

Enameled bronze Coat of arms saved from 1960s court building

4.1.14 BRISTOL CIVIL JUSTICE CENTRE

The site is located in the pre-medieval township of Redcliffe, which became a riverside suburb of Bristol in the 13th Century. Development of the densely occupied urban area intensified, with the original residential use reducing to become a mercantile and craft quarter. The characteristic medieval plot widths and street pattern became consumed and enlarged by later Georgian and Victorian commercial development. The whole area was badly damaged during the air raids of December 1940 and Post-War regeneration resulted in low value light industrial and warehousing uses. Prior to the construction of the new Bristol Civil Justice centre, 2 Redcliff Street was used as a surface car park. This was a hugely inappropriate setting for the medieval Grade 2* listed Church of St. Thomas the Martyr that overlooked the site.

The new courts development has provided a large public riverside piazza, with the courts forming one long side, an historic warehouse forming the other long side and the church dominating the far end so that after two centuries it can once again be seen from the river. Flooding was a major concern, overcome by raising the ground floor over a tanked basement, whilst providing a sloping piazza to ensure ease of access for all.

The simple 5 storey building with 9 courts and 6 hearing rooms has a civic presence with the tall highly glazed ground floor, and a subtle interplay of the grid of the structural frame with the grid of windows for the upper floors, capped by a glazed penthouse. There are echoes of the form, materials and proportions of the warehouses of Redcliffe, which is highly appropriate to the regeneration of this historic waterside quarter. The use of red sandstone (from which the red cliffs of the river, that gave the area its name, are formed) is a masterstroke.

The courts, church and public square

View from river,   detail of red sandstone facade

Interior of offices

Typical hearing room

4.1.15 CITY OF WESTMINSTER MAGISTRATES' COURT

The City of Westminster magistrates' court is located on a prominent key urban site fronting both the brash noisy urban dual carriageway of the Marylebone flyover and also the quiet elegant conservation area of the late 18th century Portman Estate. The site is awkwardly shaped and very challenging, being hemmed in by the surviving parts of the oldest court building in London, by the rights of light from the Chinese Embassy, and by the charming residential mews of Shilibeer Place. The area was run-down and unpleasant with derelict property to the rear and one of the most polluted environments in London to the front. From this unpromising start the architects have produced an elegant, urbane civic building that welcomes the public from Marylebone Road, which is now becoming a European style civic boulevard. This has been done by preserving the historic buildings and mature trees, by giving space to observe and appreciate the neighbouring high quality architecture, by removing the tawdry 1960s office blocks and empty sites and replacing them with a building that defines the urban space in its form and exudes the quality of traditional craftsmanship in natural stone in its detail.

Internally the architects have, within a complex site, produced a building of excellent clarity. It is a built diagram of how a court building should work. From the busy street the public pass through a calming courtyard before entering the welcoming glassy entrance. Inside everything is immediately laid out before you, so that the building can be understood. An atrium rises up from the ground floor security and reception area the full height of the building, showing the simple rows of 4 courts per floor fronted by waiting areas overlooking the atrium. The waiting areas calm the users in their inevitable stressful situation by giving them quiet, calming views of the bustle of life outside amongst the boulevard trees. The views outside and the dramatic space are given a quiet foil of simple finishes – white plastered walls, smooth fair-faced concrete ceilings, white ceramic floors, sparkly glass and stainless steel fittings and areas of simple natural walnut cladding to soften the acoustics. To enter the courtrooms you pass over a bridge spanning the lightwell that illuminates the courtrooms. The courtrooms themselves are simple light spaces utilising the same palette of materials.

The multitude of other various functions within a court building is cleverly kept within the poché created by the rectilinear diagram of the courts sitting within the awkward geometry of the site. The consultation rooms are within the small preserved historic court building. The offices are behind the stone screen that redefines the formerly fractured external streetscape of Marylebone Road. The retiring rooms, with their more intimate scale, terminate the quiet mews of Shillibeer Place. The custody area is in the basement, wrapping round the ancient basement of the historic court and utilising the void of the long demolished subterranean Pompeiian baths.

Overall this is an excellent example of a public building not only functioning well within itself, but also enhancing the urban environment. There are a few regrets, such as the enabling social housing to the rear failing to keep the retained elegant stucco façade of the domestic scale Regency Pompeiian baths. However the new building itself, and the life and bustle it brings to this reviving area of London, show that public architecture can be more than just frugal and functional, it can help to regenerate the inner city, utilising the most unpromising of sites to show what is possible with a keen client and a talented design team.

Westminster magistrates' court main façade and entrance forecourt

View along Marylebone Road with court offices in foreground

Courthall and atrium giving natural light to courtrooms; courtroom interior

Pompeiian baths, now sadly lost;   conserved historic courts

Main entrance and atrium;   carved stone coat of arms

4.1.16 Chelmsford magistrates' court

Sometimes a building designs itself. The Court Standards Design Guide gives ideal groupings of courtrooms and spacial relationships, an astute M&E engineer will realise the key to natural light and ventilation is the section, a tight site will dictate the fit on site, and planning restrictions such as a Conservation Area will to a certain extent dictate materials and elements of form, such as massing, roof treatment and street frontage treatment.

Chelmsford is an example of this. The site is in the heart of this historic town, in a Conservation Area. It therefore has to be on the street line, with an arcade. It has to step down in its elevation to acknowledge the 4 storey Georgian buildings and the 2 storey medieval inn on the other side, which nicely accommodates the odd number of pairs of courts (4 below, 2 above). The rectangular site with a row of trees at the rear fits perfectly for the standard linear layout. The quiet and green space to the rear dictates the orientation of the section for sustainability and functionality.

This just leaves the architect to provide some elegant brick detailing, some pavement edge columns that will not put the building and users at risk from an errant vehicle, and some airy and calming interior spaces. It is a fine result.

Main frontage

Detail of finishes; building steps to reflect context

New courts within rebuilt medieval street pattern

4.1.17 Colchester

Colchester is an ancient town. It is the highest navigable point on the river so the Romans built a quay, and founded the town on a dry defensible slope with a road on a ridge of land linking the two. In medieval times an abbey was founded outside the town walls to exploit the harbour and the trade of the town. The road on the ridge became lined with merchants' houses. In the 19th century the railway was built up the valley to exploit the harbour and town and the station was built where the road met the town.

The site of the court is exactly at the point where the high road from the harbour dips into the valley which acted as the moat to the town. It faces the ruins of the Abbey and sits on the railway sidings by the station. The site is therefore very critical to the design. The site has a long climbing frontage to the harbour road, which is lined with medieval and Georgian buildings (though spoilt by a huge traffic junction), and falls steeply to rail tracks at the rear elevation which overlooks the abbey and roman town.

Court buildings functionally tend to have two principle levels: A lower custody level where defendants are delivered via a secure van dock, from where they are led up into the courtrooms, and an upper level for the public and courtrooms to exploit the natural light and views. The fall across the site and an existing retaining wall naturally led to the cells being in the lower semi- basement level and the public entering off the historic street into the courthall and courtrooms. Perversely the designers decided to have the custody van dock at the highest point of the site, requiring a high level yard on stilts and a lift down to the cells then back up again to the courts. Equally perversely the public entrance is at the lowest level, so the entrance gets no natural light, and visitors have to walk down a steep hill and ramp to enter, then climb back up a staircase to the first floor courts at ground level.

Functionally it is illogical and the custody yard prevents the gaps in the medieval and Georgian street frontage from being repaired and infilled to restore the townscape damaged by the traffic engineers. It is a lost opportunity. However, when viewed as a piece of architecture, and once the lost opportunities are forgotten, it is quite a nice building. The overall massing is probably about right. The prominent bronze tower on St Botolph's Square with the low diminishing tail winding up the hill works well. The bronze tower is the key element of the building, It is the three dimensional front elevation onto the square, facing the historic station building. The rest is just background.

The tower marks the presence of the courts from all directions – the town, the ring road, the abbey, the railway. The entrance is obvious, and cleverly avoids the noise of both the railway and the road by being on neither frontage. It is on the tip of the site and delineates with the station a new urban square. When the sun catches the bronze tower suddenly this little bit of townscape is magical, and the perversities of planning are forgotten.

Elevation with tower and tail to harbour road

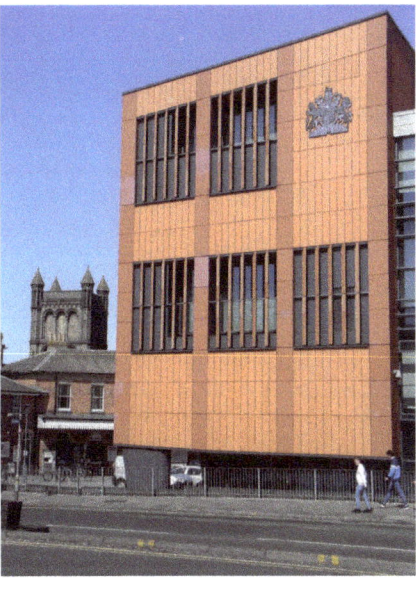

Tower in the station forecourt; tower from traffic junction with abbey beyond

Main entrance

Golden copper arts centre, inspiration for copper tower

4.1.18 Newport magistrates' court

The court scheme at Newport started out as a Government pump priming exercise to initiate the regeneration of the derelict docks of this South Wales coal port. The promise of investment successfully encouraged others to invest, but due to funding delays the scheme now on site is the last building to be built in the regeneration zone, rather than the first.

The site is set back from the banks of the tidal mudflats of the river estuary, with views to and from the river over a preserved historic dock inlet. The surroundings were originally desolate and empty, but are now fully built up with rather tawdry and uninspiring rendered blockwork office blocks. The courthouse therefore primarily addresses the river and the dramatic views from the Newport cable stayed bridge sailing overhead at almost touching distance, whilst also bringing a human scale to the surroundings through extensive landscaping once people approach the building.

The building is a simple hard brick cube sitting on a soft sculpted mound, to give a presence from the river and the bridge. The bricks are a dark brown clay with shimmering petrol blue highlights from the local coal measure clays, which were traditionally worked as a side line to the coal mining, and shipped out as floor tiles from these docks. The user friendly landscaping, using local rural dry stone walling and native tree species, is there to cope with the levels required by the flood risk of the site and to give a civic public presence and sense of arrival from the spine road and from the historic pedestrian routes from the town centre.

Visually the walls are immensely thick to emphasise the solidity, as the punched window reveals to the courtrooms actually penetrate over the perimeter judicial corridors. Viewed from the bridge above, the grass roof merges with the trees planted to muffle the road noise. Once you enter the cube through the glazed fissure of the entrance, the space suddenly opens up. There is a 17m high volume as a noise buffer zone with views up to the dramatic George St bridge and all the floor levels laid out in section before you as platforms and ramps like a quarry face, to make the building instantly understandable.

This is a small jewel of a building which punches above its (very heavy) weight.

Main frontage

High level view from Newport cable stayed bridge

Night view of brick cube

Great stair from entrance; glass cube hanging over stair

Courtroom interiors

Courtroom interior with dock   *Courtroom skylight detail*

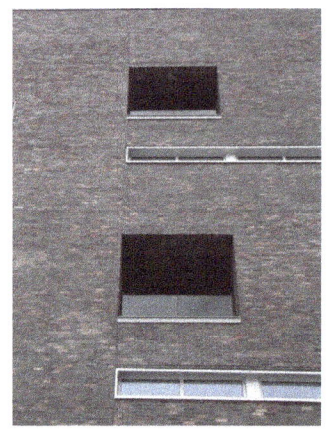

Deep recessed window detai

Wall and gabion plinth detail;   Coal-measure brick detail

4.2 Restored, extended, reused courts

4.2.1 Manchester Minshull St Crown Court

This is a model for how a redundant court building can be brought back to beneficial use in an excellent manner. The Florentine Gothic police court building had an excellent location in the centre of Manchester, and there was a small plot to the rear allowing extension. It had a simple U shaped plan with an entrance block on the street frontage and two wings of courts to the rear, with a courtyard between them. By adding new courtrooms on the ends of the wings and exploiting the existing courtyard to create an atrium the planning was rationalised to permit modern functioning as a major new Crown Court complex. The planning logic of the existing building was extended but reversed so that the public enter directly into the atrium, off which all the courts lead. The best of the Victorian spaces were brought back into use and the modern requirements for offices space, services and circulation were housed in the extension. Considerable re-ordering of the fittings was required, but even redundant architectural features such as stained glass windows have been reused in the new spaces.

It sounds simple, but there were many challenges. The long side elevation had a frontage falling straight into a canal, so a new bridge had to be built to get custody vehicles into the custody area under the atrium. This historic elevation had been opened up by the removal of adjacent warehouses, so the new extension, which was visually just one more of the repeating bays, had to be designed in the gothic style, albeit in a subtly modernised way.

The result is an excellent building, the fine airy original courtrooms were restored and he logical planning extended, whilst the circulation and public areas were turned from a maze of gloomy corridors into a relaxing and stunning atrium. The building originally had only one elevation visible and that was onto a back street. The new building has transformed the area, with a new entrance frontage just off Piccadilly, one side elevation now forming the elevation to a public garden square, rather than a back alley, and the long hidden canal-side elevation now fronting the newly opened up canal-side development area of hotels and restaurants around the railway station.

Canalside elevation: historic (l) and new extension (r);   new entrance

Historic Minshull St elevation;   corner tower

North elevation onto new park;   original main entrance

Carved gothic beasts are everywhere – dragon, griffin and owls

New atrium; reused stained glass

Rooms converted to courtrooms

New courtroom in extension; stained glass detail

Restored courtroom

Restored judicial corridor

Historic courtroom with transparent secure dock

New judge's chambers created in attic

Restored light fitting; preserved clock tower interior

4.2.2 Dundee Sheriff court

Dundee Sheriff court looks like a courthouse – a proper stern symmetrical classical building with a columned portico, dominating the end of the main civic street of this hard, dour, serious, business-like town. But all is not as it seems – both in the town and the courthouse. Dundee is not as dour and serious as it looks. Behind the façade Dundee is the home of the British comics industry – the Beano and the Dandy. Its industry is bizarrely based on a local supply of cork and oranges (for linoleum and marmalade) and it is the world centre of the raspberry industry.

Behind the formal front to the Sheriff court, the building has been transformed. Yes there is an historic courtroom, beautifully restored, but behind what were the blank screen walls are now well lit elegant courtrooms and all the necessary requirements of a modern court building. The architectural detailing cleverly enhances and lifts both the historic and modern architectural aspects of the building.

Scotland does not have the pressure to centralise justice in large city centre justice complexes, since the population is less dense than in England and the topography makes travel across country slow. Dundee is therefore the ideal model for the modern medium sized court building for the less urbanised parts of the UK.

"A proper stern symmetrical classical building with a columned portico, dominating the end of the main civic street of this hard, dour, serious, business-like town"; the new extensions peep over the historic blank flank walls

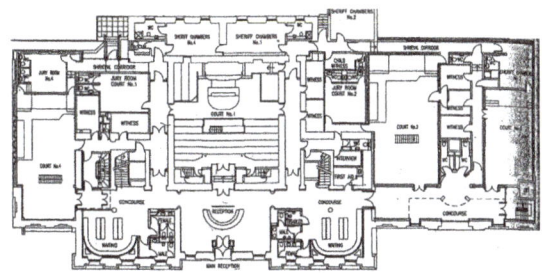

Additional courtrooms flanking historic courtroom

4.2.3 Derby

Derby Magistrates' court is one of the most important, innovative and successful re-uses of an historic building in Britain. It deserves to be more widely known.

The original building was built in 1659, after Cromwell's death near the end of the Commonwealth, and is probably the earliest surviving purpose designed law court. It is a great hall in a "heavy mannerist" English Baroque style, which originally had furniture for a pair of "Crown" and Nisi Prius" courts, one at each end with surviving separate entrance doors. The building also held the usual array of plays, gambling, dances and concerts when the courts were not sitting, which were permitted once again at the Restoration of the Monarchy.

Over the years the complex grew. A grand jury room was built to the rear in 1770. An hotel (1798) and judges' lodging (1808) were built either side to create a courtyard at the front. In 1828 new courtrooms and service wings were built at the rear and the great hall opened up and redesigned with a classical interior. In 1881 more new courtrooms and other extensions were added to the rear, after partial demolition of earlier extensions.

These rear areas were much altered until the courts closed in 1985, after which the site lay empty for 15 years. It appeared that there was just a fine but quirky old façade on a largely Victorian building.

The fact that the building was empty and that there were extensive later extensions to the rear enabled the bold and dramatic re-use. The best parts were kept: the 1659 great hall and forecourt, the Georgian hotel and judges' lodging, the early 19th century courtrooms. The warren of late 19th century accretions at the rear were demolished.

The set piece of the forecourt leading to the great hall, off which lead the courtrooms, is the core of the new building, as it has been for over 350 years. But now the great hall leads up to a top lit horse shoe courthall that encircles the historic core and feeds into a ring of excellent modern courtrooms. The planning is eminently simple, giving a natural flow for users. The clever use of site levels and internal levels means that the ancillary functions and custody are hidden below the courts or utilise the poché created between the horseshoe of courts and the more rectangular site perimeter.

It is the quality of the spaces that is so rewarding. The courtrooms have a light airy functionality, with unframed floor to ceiling glass docks, simple white finishes with a touch of wood panelling, and most importantly an elegant modelled ceiling detail giving excellent relaxing quality of light.

The courthall is the best space. The formerly hidden rear wall to the 19th century courts now forms the inner wall of the horseshoe courthall. The rooflights at the wall junction give a wall-washer effect, picking up the texture, colour and character of the old masonry, to contrast with the white simplicity of the rest of the space. The most astonishing detail is where the horseshoe meets the end of the great hall. Two huge lunette windows at either end of the great hall were revealed during the demolition of the Victorian extensions. They are original to the 1659 building, and were bricked up, plastered over and totally hidden by the 1798 remodelling, so had not been seen for over 200years. What was once external is now internal. The window cill is now a bench seat in the courthall, and the window gives astonishing views from the 21st century courthall through the Cromwellian window down into the Georgian ballroom interior of the great hall.

This is the perfect example of a building where the juxtaposition and reuse of the old and the new gives a far better building than either the new or the old would have done by themselves.

1659 facade

1798 Georgian wing and forecourt

New horseshoe of courts meets old building; 1828 classical ballroom with 1659 lunette windows

1659 great hall with new glass security pods

Window into ballroom

Restored Victorian courtroom

New courthall

Courthall detail with exposed stone walls and modern glass detailing

4.2.4 Liverpool Community Court

Liverpool Community Court was an experiment in new ways of carrying out justice, inspired by a pioneering precedent in New York. The concept was that in a depressed area of inner city Liverpool local street crime and domestic crime would be handled locally so that the community could see that justice was being done for the local community. The hope was that this perception would reduce local crime and revitalise the area by changing the perception that the area and community had been abandoned to crime. Justice would be at the centre of the community, in the community centre.

The building had to be provided quickly to exploit the high profile impetus of the Political announcement. A suitable building had to be found for conversion in the heart of the community concerned. A fine Victorian library was rejected as being too "establishment", a vandalised retail shed was rejected as being too prone to vandalism, and a church hall was rejected since a popular boxing club would have to move. A former school was chosen since it was due to close imminently and had the advantage of providing both outdoor and indoor community facilities as well as the court.

The original form of the 1950s school was extracted from later alterations and emphasised to exploit its low key elegance. The inside was gutted, opened up and reorganised for the new functions. After initial opposition from some sections of the local populace (potential customers?), the community gradually realised the benefits of this positive idea, and came round to positively supporting it, as a way of changing the status quo for the better.

New entrance to community court

Courtroom

Rear elevation of former school

4.2.5 Guernsey

The Royal Court on Guernsey is where all Guernsey law courts and their parliament sit. It also archives the records of property ownership, marriages and company records, and accommodates all probation, custody and law officers. It holds weddings and all the ceremonies of state. The site lies within St Peter Port's conservation area and the existing historic Royal Court is listed.

The new courts reuse much of the historic prison building that was part of the complex, particularly the massive granite walls. There is a steep fall across the site, which is exploited to make the best use of the levels. In principle the circulation is in a sliver of atrium cut through the complex, utilising a former road, which gives access to all new and old elements from various street levels and rationalises the whole complex. About 75% of the historic stone arched cells were taken down, and the stone arches reused in the restoration and alteration.

The historic courts became the civil courts, and the new courts are the criminal courts. Interestingly, the criminal courts do not have a jury in the legal system of this tiny independent island, instead elder statesmen acts as jurats, in a system apparently predating the reforms of the English legal system by Henry II in the twelfth century. Not all is ancient however, the Guernsey courts use electronic evidence, long before it becomes common in English courts.

The resulting building complex in its dramatic context is a superb example of how new and old can be combined by talented architects to produce a stunning piece of architecture to enhance the environment and benefit functionality.

Main entrance into new atrium; general view of Royal Court complex

Guernsey coat of arms

Interior of restored historic court room

Remains of prison cells

New circulation atrium; external view of new wing

4.2.6 Gee Street civil courthouse

The Gee Street courthouse in Clerkenwell, London, is a unique and innovative idea for a County Court. Usually new county courts are squeezed, more or less successfully, into standard office buildings. All the developer's fit out has to be stripped out and thrown away – suspended ceilings, services, toilets, reception, etc. – and the courts end up with poor natural light and inefficient circuitous circulation. At Gee St a sturdy old factory was converted. The shell of the 5 storey 1930s glass merchant (later an HMSO publication store) had been restored for light industrial use, so there was no fit-out to throw away. The floors were a deep plan, with a simple column grid and acres of glazing. Not only was this warehouse much cheaper than a modern office building, it lent itself to a much simpler and better conversion.

The wonderfully chunky and crude concrete columns form a recurring design feature. The simple white painted concrete and brick walls give a robust character throughout. The huge steel industrial windows give a wonderful quality of light into the courtrooms, judges' offices and public spaces. It is to the senior judiciary's credit that they could perceive the possibilities of such an industrial building, when they were used to the gothic grandeur of buildings such as the Royal Courts of Justice, and this was well before Clerkenwell became fashionable for the studios of the design industry. For the judges, it is now one of the most popular London courts in which to work.

General view of 1930s building; main entrance; entrance hall

Stair; judge's bathroom

Office with distinctive column; general office

Attic courtroom; courtroom

Large courtroom

Small courtroom

4.2.7 Hendon

The original Hendon magistrates' court is a small symmetrical late Victorian brick Queen Anne style edifice sitting on an elevated plot behind fine specimen pine trees. It could easily be mistaken for a rural vicarage, if it were not perched above a busy urban dual carriageway surrounded by retail sheds, Chinese takeaways and pound shops.

The brief was to triple the size and make the courts more accessible without having to climb the 39 steps to the front door. The solution was to build a new simple modern building next door, which neither tried to imitate the last vestige of Victoriana in the area, nor sank to the low standards of the adjacent tin sheds. The two buildings are linked together with a simple glazed link, which resolves the circulation problems and the multiple levels, whilst giving some quirky detailed views of the old (and formerly hidden) side elevation as you climb the stairs.

The external levels are resolved by the simple expedient of providing a winding sloping path through the wooded gardens from a repositioned original gateway up to a new entrance terrace. From here users can relax and view the bustle and noise of the street down below, before bracing themselves for the stress of the court hearing in either one of the charming restored courts, with their scumble glazed woodwork, or one of the airy and calming new courts.

Main frontage – new and old – at-grade entrance on right

New extension; louvred end of new extension; detail of new extension

New entrance with re-used gates

New court room; historic painted courtroom

Historic fittings being refinished; interface between new and old

4.2.8 Supreme Court

The Supreme Court in Parliament Square, London, is a replacement for the courtrooms in the House of Lords (for the Law Lords) and in Downing Street (for the Judicial Committee of the Privy Council). It houses the most senior courts of appeal for the UK and for the Commonwealth, and was established to separate the Judiciary from the Legislature, to avoid any possibility of a suggestion of Political influence over the judiciary.

The brief was for 3 hearing rooms, a vast library of precedent, chambers for each of the judges, plus all the usual public space and offices, and, innovatively, facilities for the public to observe and understand the proceedings. There was a strict requirement that it had to be located no more than 10 minutes walk from the House of Lords. The Law Lords (now known modestly as Justices) were very precise clients. They do not accept compromise in their judicial decisions and they would not accept compromise in the design.

A range of buildings and sites were considered: the west wing of Somerset House on the Strand (too far away), the Old War Office in Whitehall (too large), the Office of the Parliamentary Advocate General in Whitehall (too small), a site in Buckingham Gate (not prominent enough), County Hall (wrong side of the river). Middlesex Guildhall in Parliament Square was initially considered too gothic, and symbolically too much like the House of Lords, so not modern enough to symbolise the innovative and forward looking attitudes of the Supreme Court.

Ultimately everyone realised the building was ideal. It was the right size, there were three fine large rooms for hearing rooms, there was an entire wing that had been gutted of all floors and walls in the 1960s so could have entirely new accommodation. The perfect symbolism of the four sides of Parliament Square being the four corners of a civilised society: the Legislature (Houses of Parliament), the Government (The Treasury Building), the Church (Westminster Abbey) and the Judiciary (Supreme Court), finally sealed the selection of the former Middlesex Guildhall.

The building was built in 1906 in a flamboyant mixture of Gothic and Arts & Crafts styles. Knowing that Middlesex was likely to be become defunct as a County and subsumed into Greater London, it appears that the council spent all its remaining reserves on a monument to the history and craftsmanship of London, Middlesex and Justice. (Middlesex had for a thousand years been the home of the Magna Carta at Runnymede, The Royal Courts of Justice and Parliament.)

The guildhall originally had two grand formal courtrooms and a council chamber in the centre of the building, flanked by lightwells and surrounded by offices and reception rooms facing all four street frontages. The lightwells had been filled in over the years, making the building dark and gloomy, made worse by overgrown trees burying the front elevation.

The lightwells were reopened and extended down into the basement. The much altered council chamber was re-ordered as a hearing room. One exquisite historic courtroom was restored. The central courtroom, which had been rather squat but with a magnificent Edwardian baroque ceiling, was extended downwards to create a multi level library (inspired by the set of the film "The Name of the Rose") and opened out into the entrance hall to symbolise the library as the heart of the Supreme Court. The wing facing Westminster Abbey, which had had additional floors inserted in the 1960s, was re-formed as a thoroughly modern double height courtroom opening onto a balcony overlooking Westminster Abbey. To enhance the main frontage, various wild ideas for sunken plazas and crystalline porticos were dreamt up (by Norman Foster), but then dismissed in favour of something more subtle and successful – pruning back the belt of trees, cleaning the façade, and replacing the service road with an arc of poetical seating from where to contemplate the meaning of the historic narrative sculptures of the origins of justice.

The detailing of the new work is as astonishing as the historic craftsmanship. Elegant and erudite quotations are inscribed to contrast with baroque plasterwork. Witty giant floral chintz (by Wee Timorous Beasties) drape beside a sarcastic sculpture of Lloyd George as a moneybags Chancellor of the Exchequer. Pop Art carpets by Peter Blake sear the eyes next to virulent original acid green wall tiles.

Middlesex Guildhall has finally found its true calling. It never really worked as a town hall or a law court. It makes a magnificent Supreme Court, completing the fourth side of Parliament Square, with the architecture symbolising the continuity of justice and the daring rethinking of the details echoing the new thinking in each new decision of the Justices of the Supreme Court.

Main frontage to Parliament Square; side elevation facing Westminster Abbey

Library

Main stair

Judicial stair with Peter Blake's pop art carpet and original acid green tiles

New court room facing Westminster Abbey

Lloyd George sculpture;   *Café with giant carpet pattern*

Waiting area

Waiting area ceiling and lighting

Library ceiling

External sculpture detail

Courtroom detail; small courtroom

Furniture detail; Main courtroom – former council chamber

Entrance hall with engraved glass screen

4.2.9 Isleworth Crown court

Isleworth Crown court was originally a conversion of a wartime prefabricated hospital located within a grand west London suburb of substantial Victorian houses set within well wooded grounds. The area had seen better days but had just been declared a Conservation Area. When a substantial extension was required to accommodate the Crown courts displaced from Middlesex Guildhall (for the Supreme Court), the opportunity was taken to to upgrade the whole complex and provide a building more appropriate to the Conservation Area.

The new extension is a free standing, unashamedly modern building, replacing in form, scale, materials and detailing, a long lost villa in its grand sylvan circus setting. It effectively masks the ramshackle older single storey buildings, whilst functionally extending and terminating the simple linear plan of the existing complex. The mature landscaping forms an excellent setting, and the wooded views and landscaped courtyards give excellent calming views from inside the courts, public spaces and judges' retiring rooms.

New pavilion building amongst the trees of the circus

Extensions within the grounds

Sliver of atrium; circulation core of new building

View from new to old

Waiting area; WW2 hospital converted to courts

4.2.10 Aberystwyth Justice Centre

Aberystwyth Justice Centre has probably one of the finest locations of any court building. It sits on the quay side overlooking the Y Llanfa marina with all the courtrooms, offices and public areas having magnificent views out to sea with the yachts and fishing boats of the harbour in the foreground and the whole view framed by the castle, old town and surrounding hills capped by the University. The users can go mackerel fishing from the boat moored outside and barbecue their catch on the judges' terrace.

This is about as far as you can get from an inner city magistrates' court catering for what some people perceive as "the losers in life". It is also just about as far and remote as you can get when heading west. It is 4 hours over the mountains from the next nearest court. But don't be fooled by perceptions. Virtually its first case was a horrendous case of child kidnap, rape and murder. Crime is no respecter of location or beauty and inner city squalor is no requirement for crime. Justice is required everywhere and for everyone.

It has two formal courtrooms, and three versatile hearing rooms for use by youth courts, civil courts and tribunals. It is a few minutes walk from the train station (one train every two hours, but only in the summer) and the town centre, and is at the hub of the local road network, so fulfils its technical requirements. Originally it had been intended to have a new PFI scheme the preferred site for which was on a site on an industrial estate overlooking the railway sidings a couple of miles from the town centre, which was hardly ideal, and which ended up under water during the 2012 Welsh floods. This was dropped when the cost drifted over £15m. The Y Llanfa courts, with the same brief, were built for £3m, (including, land, fees and VAT). Astonishingly it is one of the cheapest new courts in the country, as well as one of the most charming.

Architecturally the style could be called "seaside jolly", with quirky additions clearly taken from the vernacular of the working quayside buildings of the fishing fleet. There may even be a nod to New England vernacular from the American architects. In reality it is an extension and conversion of a 1990s quayside office and chandlery building, but you would never guess. The entrance was moved from the waterside to the landward side, since with a westerly storm blowing you could not open the original front door nor even stand up in the face of the wind. The previous building was almost doubled in width to provide the necessary lifts, stairs and custody van dock, and this cleverly enabled the open floor plates of the former offices to be used for the courtrooms and public spaces, making the best use of the magnificent views. The use of the new lift tower capped with the royal coat of arms symbolically expresses from afar the civic function of the building. Appropriately the tower echoes the tower of the Library of Wales that can be seen dominating the adjacent hilltop, and which holds the ancient original copies of the 9th century Laws of Hywel Dda, which preceded the introduction of English Law to Wales.

Courts from the sea wall; entrance tower

General view in context

Landward elevation from under bridge; courtroom

4.2.11 Sunderland magistrates' court

Sunderland was historically a small town founded by monks on the cliffs above the gorge of the river Wear. In 1801 it had a population of 12,412. The population of Sunderland soared in the 19th century and by 1901 it had risen to 146,000, as a result of coal and ship building, and the bridging of the gorge. The magistrates' courts were built in 1905 at the height of the boom as part of a civic complex on a busy corner opposite the Vaux brewery, next door to the police station and market hall with the fire station to the rear. They are built in local stone ashlar with roof of graduated slates in Free Baroque style. The formerly hidden rear elevations are in very plain utilitarian red brick. There are two large formal jury courts with a Grand Jury room on an upper level between them, presumably with the intention of becoming Assize courts, though they are still signed as Police courts.

The town went into decline in the 1930s, and has never really recovered. The police station was demolished and rebuilt in 1973 for road widening, exposing the former courtyard elevation, originally entered under the clock tower. The front of the court building became a major traffic intersection, cutting it off from the town centre. The fire station and market hall behind were closed, and the whole area was proposed for redevelopment. A large new court building on an adjacent site was proposed, which would have included a new Crown court and the civil courts. When this scheme was abandoned after 2008 the existing courts and their urban setting we rethought.

The long disused Grand Jury room was converted into a fine vaulted court room. The historic courtrooms were restored. The County Court and tribunals moved in, utilising additional small modern hearing rooms created in former offices, based on the latest ideas of versatile minimal utilitarian hearing rooms for civil, criminal and tribunal cases. In 2015 the facades were cleaned and restored to reveal their hidden grandeur, the busy road was moved and public squares with fountains and gardens were created in front of the courts to revitalise the city centre and tie the historic fabric of the city back to the long lost river gorge.

Main frontage onto new piazza with fountain

Grand jury room converted to court room

Restored historic court room

Office converted to new hearing room

Restored entrance tower; coat of arms in judicial corridor

Formerly hidden side elevation, now facing garden square

4.3 Courts to come and the ones that got away

4.3.1 ABERYSTWYTH MILL ST SCHEME

One of the other PDS schemes for Aberystwyth was on an important infill site in the heart of the town. Mill Street is an historic street leading from the town centre to the historic river crossing. It is a mixed commercial and residential back street, dominated by the rear of a huge and very austere chapel, dated 1785.

The frontage has a 4m drop that would have accommodated vehicle and custody entry at a lower ground level, with a pedestrian entry on the upper ground level on Mill Street. Due to the historic urban character of Mill Street the street frontage formed a continuation of the existing frontage line. Upper floors would have had views to the harbour and beyond to the sea.

The solution from the local architects was a very sensitive infill scheme, restoring the integrity of this ancient street damaged by unthinking demolition some years ago. This was a model of urban infill. It exploited the site characteristics and was of a scale appropriate to a small street in the medieval part of the largely Victorian seaside town.

Unfortunately, whilst the site could be excellent for a court building, the local authority's insistence on incorporating a multi-storey car park as well as the courts on this site made the scheme too expensive and compromised the functionality of the courts.

4.3.2 BRADFORD MAGISTRATES' COURT

The reason for a new magistrates' court in Bradford is quite surreal. Bradford was a city in decline. Two thirds of the city centre was empty and derelict, meaning that any development could not be commercially viable. The town master-planners proposed to remove the bulk of the wasteland and create a core of a town that was smaller but commercially viable and an attractive place in which to live, to shop and to do business. Over half the town would be grassed over or turned into a vast lake in a natural bowl, very similar to that of Sienna. The lake would be a reflecting pool for the stunning historic Italian gothic town hall, and would have boating, a beach and ice cream stalls, and would be surrounded by restaurants, bars and speciality shops. The town would be revived as a destination shopping venue and leisure attraction.

Unfortunately the existing 1960s police station and magistrates' court were sitting in the middle of the lake.

The police moved out to the ring road, and a new court building was proposed to enable the lake to happen and to also urbanise another critical piece of city centre wasteland. The site was on an awkward vacant plot forming the final side of a new square surrounded by an historic hotel, newspaper offices and the 1990s Crown court. There is a 3 storey fall across the site, with a railway tunnel across one corner and a huge retaining wall to the rear.

The proposed court uses the levels to achieve a lower ground floor shared custody yard, a public entrance onto the square, a first floor link to the Crown court and a 2nd floor rear entrance to the offices. An external public footpath weaves its way up from the square onto a bridge up to the rear street (and leisure centre) which leads to the historic mill quarter of the town and to the railway station.

The multiple access levels led to a design with an office wing at the rear and the public entrance to the courts off the square, with the court rooms above. The custody yard and parking are shared with the Crown court at a slightly sunken level. There was even enough space left over from the compact efficient plan to squeeze in some commercial development and permit the old railway tunnel to be kept for a future tram link.

The classic simplicity of the elevation belies the complexity inside and gives a calm but formal and civic side to the square, whilst trying not to compete with the more dramatic or historic buildings on the other sides of the square.

With the decline of the magistrates' court workload, the magistrates eventually shared the modified 1980s Crown Court next door.

4.3.3 Aylesbury Crown Court

The existing Aylesbury Crown Court was in a much mutilated Georgian town hall building which faced onto the town square and used to be the frontage to a long closed prison. The intention was to combine Aylesbury with other local Crown Court buildings.

The proposed court was a deceptively simple building. It had a straight long trabeated almost Classical frontage of columns on a stepped plinth with a cornice. The site sits at the top of a long hill the old road of which descends from the railway down to the town centre, so that it dominates the approach to the historic market town. The adjacent medieval cottages and regency town houses indicate that this was the earliest of suburbs to the market town in the valley below.

The simplicity was carefully developed from a highly complex site and brief. The site is a quadrant on a road junction that cut the site off from the context. There is a very steep fall across the site, so the rear is over a storey below the street frontage. The only site vehicle access is from a side road winding down to the lower part of the site. Concern over the scale has been expressed, but it clearly derives from the Regency terraces which once were the character of the main road.

The simplicity expresses itself in the pure and classic linear arrangement of courts all one level, with the court hall in front. This is a perfect model of the standard diagram for courts.

4.3.4 Snaresbrook crown court

Snaresbrook Crown Court was built as a school in the 19th century, with extensive grounds overlooking Epping Forest and a large formal lake (Eagle Pond) distancing it from the town centre. It was originally gutted and converted in the 1960s and has had a number of "temporary" extensions over the years since then. The area has been improving, with the adjacent noisy and busy A12 trunk road recently put into a tunnel under the heath.

The new extension will add 8 new courtrooms on the footprint of the dilapidated single storey rear extensions. The plan layout of the existing building is rationalised to integrate with the new extensions, so that the entire building will work more simply and logically. The custody, jury and waiting areas will no longer be distributed erratically around the building in multiple locations. Users are led straight from the main entrance into a restored cloister then along a broad reopened original courthall, off which are the existing courtrooms, which leads to a new airy 2 storey glass courthall facing the heath, off which open the new courtrooms.

The rear of the original building, which contained kitchens, plant, dustbin yards, and temporary sheds, despite being the principal frontage viewed from the public heath and woodland of Epping Forest, will now be an elegant and formal frontage in its own right. Users of the heath will no longer have a grand view of a dustbin yard, and users of the courts will at last get views out to appreciate the stunning and calming landscape setting, rather than views into the internal service yards and lightwells.

4.3.5 West Bromwich magistrates' court

The West Bromwich design is a pleasant simple 2 storey building containing four top lit courts either side of a central courthall on the first floor, with the entrance and custody on the ground floor. It has an over-sailing gull-wing roof giving a civic presence at the top of the main shopping street and welcome shelter from the rain. Its interest lies in the novel and excellent way the offices are handled.

The site is flat and bland amongst derelict factories and wasteland. The entire town is in fact, sadly, largely the derelict factories and wasteland of the former industrial heartland of the Birmingham conurbation. It is a town full of dreams - they dream of a new college, a new shopping centre, a new art centre, new luxury housing, but none of them come to fruition. One of its most recent new buildings was an industrial shed, but that has been demolished to build the courts.

The courts, and the significant office accommodation for the region, were intended to bring new business to the area. It would have been a convenient location to work, located next to the shops and cafes of the town centre, and conveniently close to the rail station and parking, with an excellent new road infrastructure.

The notable feature of the offices was that they were in a deep plan well lit double height space with atria and bridges for the 1st floor elements giving open plan efficient office accommodation, but also defining informal groups of desks to differentiate the different functional teams (with their security and privacy) yet encourage working together. It was aimed at the integrated justice system developed in Nuneaton and Leamington, where all the justice agencies work together to give flowing integrated justice processes for each case, by passing the files across the desk to the next agency, rather than repeatedly sending them to another office elsewhere for processing. The office element of the design is truly innovative in this modest yet dynamic court building.

With the decline in demand, the expansion from the existing single old courtroom became unnecessary, and the magistrates moved a few miles down the road into Birmingham magistrates' court.

4.3.6 SUNDERLAND JUSTICE CENTRE

This scheme is all about exploiting the site, and the site is one of the most dramatic imaginable. Astonishingly it is also just about the cheapest site that MoJ has purchased for a court building. It is on top of a steep cliff overlooking a deep cleft of a valley running down from the Sunderland plateau into the gorge of the River Wear. The drama is emphasised by a huge stone retaining wall forming the site edge, like that of a Japanese castle.

The view from the site down the valley is framed by the slender footbridge of a former railway spanning from plateau to plateau. The valley is something out of the wilds of Northumberland with dry stone walls enclosing tiny fields in the valley bottom, and oak scrub on the steep valley flanks. Astonishingly, at the top it leads straight into the shops and cathedral of the town centre in a bizarre juxtaposition.

The site is worthy of Frank Lloyd Wright, and thankfully the architect probably knows more about FLW than any other English architect, having restored a number of his buildings.

The design solution is a horizontal linear building along the cliff top, with the key functions and public spaces exploiting the views, to calm and relax the stressed users. The route through the building, the office area, the atrium and the landscaping all emphasise the linearity, drawing a line from the historic town centre to the edge of the gorge.

The valley is the historic reason for the town – it was the natural route from the sheltered moorings and ferry crossing in the gorge up the cliffs onto the defensible plateau. The proposed courts were to appear from below as a fortification guarding the entry to the town from the river.

The immediacy of the gorge and the town has been lost for centuries as industry took over the cliff top plateau, and the pioneering road and rail bridges spanned the gorge, leaving the pack horse route redundant. Now that the industry has gone, Sunderland is rediscovering its geographic reason for its site, and this building would have celebrated the town's location. From this public building and its gardens you could see the gorge, the valley, the town centre, the cathedral, the famous bridges over the gorge, and from the upper floors the view out to the wild North Sea.

The scheme was not pursued once the adjacent major development on the old brewery site failed to materialise, leaving the site isolated. The local authority created a major new urban square in front of the historic courts, replacing a noisy and polluting traffic junction. This made the conservation and reuse of the existing building a wise option, which has enhanced the entire area of the city.

4.3.7 Liverpool magistrates' court

The architects were presented with the site from hell on which to build this most complex of buildings. Court buildings very frequently have to use challenging sites since the easy sites in the middle of cities are sought after by developers and are therefore far too costly for the public purse.

The site was assembled from a collection of disparate but adjoining vacant plots of land. It is in a Conservation Area with Listed Buildings on all sides protruding into the site, giving a site looking like a piece from a jigsaw puzzle. Running diagonally across the site is a tunnel about 2m below the surface. Crossing below this are twin railway tunnels and a main sewer. This only left about 10% of the site where any piles could be placed, and even then, only with the utmost of care. The rear of the site linked into and looked onto a series of narrow historic lanes of small scale workshops, warehouses and pubs. The main frontage of the site was a grand Victorian street of civic buildings built to celebrate Liverpool's role as one of the greatest ports of the empire, but which now is half filled with modern office blocks.

The competition design managed to produce the ideal model – two pairs of courtrooms with the public side opening off the main road, and the private side opening off a discrete side street, adjacent to the metro station and civil courts. The structural challenges led to a highly complex organic fibrous mesh of steel to translate the logical planning grid to the erratic restricted pile locations. It echoed the organic caul wrapping of a traditional local faggot meat ball, but was unfairly compared with the Beijing Olympics "birds nest" stadium, with which it was contemporary. Liverpool was a logical and radical structural solution to a challenging site, not the affectation of an artist collaborator. It was a pity that later iterations lost its dynamism and innovation.

The varying scale of the different facades and the depth of the detail within the façade treatment echoed the quantity of detail in the ornamental Victorian facades and the vernacular textural details of the historic warehouses, whilst striving and succeeding in being radically contemporary.

The technical challenges of such a high risk site however led to a low risk decision for the magistrates to utilise spare capacity and redundant office space within the Crown court.

Liverpool magistrates' court competition design

4.3.8 Birmingham magistrates' court

Fresh from their multi-award winning success at Manchester CJC, Denton Corker Marshall were asked to tackle the challenge of putting 24 magistrates' courts on a tiny sloping sliver of city centre site in Birmingham. There were superficial similarities – a tall building within a city centre regeneration masterplan – but the differences dictated the form of the building. This was a tight traffic island site hemmed in on two sides by a busy noisy inner ring road, and hard up to high rise residential on the other sides. There were no views out, no wind to catch for ventilation, no possibility of opening windows, and no space for a grand gesture of an atrium.

The design took the curved edge of the site boundary and the tortional twist of the ground levels and extruded these into a smooth black warped rod, reminiscent of a flint nodule or perhaps appropriately the armour of the comic book hero Judge Dread. The latter inadvertent symbolism led to the severity being lightened by the addition of bright yellow boxes (windows) penetrating the slick impervious skin and erupting through the public square outside.

Internally the design was a simple arrangement of two pairs of courts in a row, with the servant space in the interstices between the rectangular courts and the curvaceous skin.

It would have been a stunning addition to Birmingham.

However, no viable alternative use for the grade 1 Listed historic court building could be found, and with some clever re-ordering of the vast underused later wings of the Victoria Law Courts, the decision was made for the courts to stay in their historic home.

5. Appendices

5.1 List of illustrations

Part 1

Fig No.

1.1. Oakham castle 1180 – the earliest form of courthouse with pre-Norman origins

1.2. Chester consistory court 1635 - the standard arrangement until the Commonwealth *(photo credit Historic England)*

1.3. Winchester Castle Assizes in 1764 with fitted furniture for civil and criminal courts at opposite ends of the Great Hall, the most common arrangement after the Restoration of the Monarchy

1.4. Warwick Shire Hall 1753 – the courtrooms are separated from the great hall by 1768

1.5. Ely Shire Hall 1821, built following Corn Law riots, has complete separation of the judiciary from the public, with all parties in fixed seating.

1.6. Gloucester Shire Hall 1815 has two semi-circular courtrooms with a continuous public gallery to observe the proceedings

1.7. Burton upon Trent county court 1862 - a typical Charles Reeves Italianate County court

1.8. The Royal Courts of Justice, London, 1874 show the arrangement of a series of courtrooms around a great hall with separate circulation for judges and advocates

1.9. Soane's Law Courts built as a series of courtrooms off Westminster Hall, with separate circulation for judges and advocates, which formed the model for all future large court complexes.

1.10. Birmingham Victoria Law courts 1891

1.11. Preston Sessions Hall 1900

1.12. Liverpool magistrates' courts 1858

1.13. Cardiff Crown court 1904

1.14. Newport Crown court 1936

1.15. Kingston on Thames Guildhall 1935

1.16.	Newcastle police court 1931	
1.17.	Harlow magistrates' court 1963	
1.18.	Leamington Spa magistrates' court 1968	
1.19.	Mold magistrates' court 1969	
1.20.	Preston combined court 1994	
1.21.	Liverpool QE2 combined court 1983	
1.22.	Bristol magistrates' court 1975	
1.23.	Northampton combined court 1991	
1.24.	Lincoln magistrates' court 1991	
1.25.	Truro crown court 1989	
1.26.	Ludlow County Court shared the magistrates' mediaeval Guildhall	
1.27.	Caernarfon Crown court moved out of the Georgian Guildhall to share with the magistrates	
1.28.	The courts from Warwick, Stratford and Leamington joined the police in a new complex in Leamington Spa	
1.29.	Bow Street magistrates' court	
1.30.	Bristol Guild Hall courts	
1.31.	The old Manchester county court	
1.32.	Bradford magistrates	
1.33.	Manchester Assize courts competition design 1862	
1.34.	Supreme Court library – balance between new and old	
1.35.	plans of courts from the CSDG 2007, ready to paste into a new design	
1.36.	multi award winning Manchester Civil Justice Centre	

PART 2 – no illustrations

PART 3

3.1.	site diagram	
3.2.	Reading Crown court – multiple new courtrooms behind historic front	
3.3.	developed site diagram	
3.4.	Bristol civil	

- 3.5. Kings Lynn Crown court in its historic quayside setting
- 3.6. Snaresbrook landscape
- 3.7. Westminster magistrates retained tree
- 3.8. Nuneaton wall
- 3.9. supreme court bench
- 3.10. Exeter crown in landscape
- 3.11. Manchester Minshull St crown court model
- 3.12. Derby courthall
- 3.13. Westminster Hall
- 3.14. York Crown
- 3.15. Lancaster Crown
- 3.16. Warwick Crown Court 1753
- 3.17. Birmingham Victoria Law Courts
- 3.18. Newport Edwardian Baroque
- 3.19. Halifax County court
- 3.20. Ilford County court
- 3.21. Rochester Row police court
- 3.22. Penzance County court
- 3.23. Barrow in Furness
- 3.24. Oxford Combined court
- 3.25. Banbury Magistrates' court
- 3.26. Liverpool QE2
- 3.27. Caernarfon Crown court extension
- 3.28. Halifax magistrates' court – the bench is in the fireplace!
- 3.29. Royal Courts of Justice, judges room
- 3.30. Rolls Building RCJ annexe – converted from office building
- 3.31. Liverpool Civil
- 3.32. Lewes Crown Court – attic converted to offices
- 3.33. Birmingham VLC clerk's desk
- 3.34. Worcester clerk's desk
- 3.35. York Crown court
- 3.36. Knutsford gasolier
- 3.37. Caernarfon stone wall

3.38. Grenoble
3.39. Newport interior
3.40. Basildon plan
3.41. Warwick leper hospital site
3.42. Southampton magistrates' court
3.43. Salford
3.44. Wolverhampton Crown Court
3.45. Westminster magistrates' court
3.46. Belfast Laganside courthall
3.47. Newcastle Quayside courts interior
3.48. Miami Dade court interior (*photo credit Arquitectonica International*)
3.49. Supreme court retiring room
3.50. Lincoln magistrates' consultation room
3.51. West Bromwich offices (*illustration credit Hurd Rolland*)
3.52. Wolverhampton offices (*illustration credit Hurd Rolland*)
3.53. Aix law courts
3.54. Caernarfon shire hall
3.55. Nuneaton justice centre
3.56. Dijon courthouse
3.57. Aberystwyth justice centre
3.58. Truro
3.59. Southwark
3.60. Peterborough
3.61. Hendon louvres
3.62. Liverpool QE2 roof plant rooms
3.63. Manchester CJC roof intakes
3.64. Truro conical roof
3.65. Newport bricks
3.66. Bournemouth interior
3.67. Manchester Civil Justice Centre view of city
3.68. Truro courthall
3.69. Hendon
3.70. Gee St courthouse

3.71. Nuneaton
3.72. Leamington coat of arms
3.73. Chester magistrates' court
3.74. Supreme court landscape
3.75. Sunderland site wall

Part 4

4.1.1. Cambridge County *(CGI credit Hurd Rolland)*
4.2.5. Guernsey *(photo credits Guernsey Royal Courts)*

5.2 Data sheet of examples

chapter No	completion date	cost per courtroom (£m)	design architect
4.1.1. Cambridge County	May-05	£1.15	Hurd Rolland Partnership
4.1.2. Manchester magistrates	May-05	£1.67	Gensler Architecture
4.1.3. Huntingdon magistrates	Sep-06	£3.6	Crampin and Pring Architects Ltd
4.1.4. Worle magistrates	Sep-06		Building Designs Partnership Ltd
4.1.5. Exeter crown	Jun-07		Jacobs Babtie
4.1.6. Bristol magistrates	Sep-07		Building Designs Partnership Ltd
4.1.7. Cambridge Crown	Oct-07		Austin Smith Lord Architects
4.1.8. Loughborough magistrates	May-08	£2.8	Stephen George & Partners
4.1.9. Cambridge magistrates	Sep-08		Siddell Gibson Architects
4.1.10 Manchester Civil Justice Centre,	Sep-08	£3.02	Denton Corker Marshall
4.1.11 Salisbury magistrates	Jun-09	£3.30	Feilden + Mawson LLP
4.1.12 Caernarfon justice centre	May-10	£4.50	HOK
4.1.13 Leamington Spa justice centre	Jul-10	£4.29	Hurd Rolland Partnership
4.1.14 Bristol Civil courts	Oct-10	£2.85	Associated Architects
4.1.15 City of Westminster magistrates	Sep-11	£3.8	Hurd Rolland Partnership
4.1.16 Chelmsford magistrates	Sep-12	£2.57	Aedas
4.1.17 Colchester magistrates	Sep-12	£3.24	Aedas
4.1.18 Newport magistrates	Sep-13	£3.3	HOK
4.2.1. Manchester Minshull Street	Sep-96		Hurd Rolland Partnership
4.2.2. Dundee Sheriff court	Sep-96	£0.74	Nicoll Russell Studios

chapter No	completion date	cost per courtroom (£m)	design architect
4.2.3. Derby magistrates	May-05		Austin Smith Lord Architects
4.2.4. Liverpool Community court	Sep-05	£2.5	Nicoll Russell Studios
4.2.5. Guernsey Royal courts	Dec-06	£2.92	Nicholas Hare Architects
4.2.6. Gee St civil courthouse	Mar-07	£0.47	HOK
4.2.7. Hendon magistrates	Sep-09	£2.84	Feilden + Mawson LLP
4.2.8. The Supreme Court	Oct-09		Feilden + Mawson LLP
4.2.9. Isleworth crown	Feb-11	£2.04	Hurd Rolland Partnership
4.2.10. Aberystwyth quay side	Sep-12	£0.6	HOK
4.2.11 Sunderland magistrates	Jun-15		Balfour Beatty
4.3.1. Aberystwyth Mill Street	Jun-06	£2.09	Powell Dobson
4.3.2. Bradford magistrates	Mar-09	£2.5	Hurd Rolland Partnership
4.3.3. Aylesbury crown	Oct-09	£8.8	HOK
4.3.4. Snaresbrook crown	Nov-09		HOK
4.3.5. West Bromwich magistrates	Mar-10	£3.8	Hurd Rolland Partnership
4.3.6. Sunderland justice centre	May-10	£3.51	John McAslan and Partners
4.3.7. Liverpool magistrates	Jun-10	£3.8	Sheppard Robson / Hurd Rolland Partnership
4.3.8. Birmingham magistrates	Jun-10	£5.33	Denton Corker Marshall

www.ingramcontent.com/pod-product-compliance
Lightning Source LLC
Chambersburg PA
CBHW040744020526
44114CB00048B/2912